The Fox Who Wondered Why

Jonathan Ank

Edited by

Michael Martin, PhD

ELEMAGICUS MEDIA

Copyright © 2025 by Elemagicus Media

All rights reserved.

No part of this publication may be copied, reproduced or used in any format, by any means, electronic or otherwise, without the prior written consent of the copyright owner and publisher of this book.

This is a work of fiction. Names, characters, places, businesses, events, and incidents are either the products of the author's imagination or used in a fictitious manner. Any resemblance to actual persons, living or dead, or actual events is purely coincidental.

The animal archetypes are symbolic literary devices designed to explore universal patterns of power and society. They are not depictions of specific real-world individuals or institutions.

Published by Elemagicus Media

Edited by Michael Martin, PhD

Cover design by Aron Visuals

Interior illustrations by Jonathan Ank

ISBN: 979-8-9942614-1-5

For my Kit:

I walked through the thorns that your steps still might choose
The pathway that asks why, not the one that woos.
I carried the flame past the Curtain they weave
To show you the thread, not the gold they believe.

Though the world may seem loud, do not fear its cry;
Let questions guide you if voices start to lie.
When you stand at the crossroads, do not give in;
Follow the warm ember that kindles within.

CONTENTS

Prologue	1
1. The Great Beginning	3
2. Kit and the Curtain	7
3. Owl's Edict	10
4. The Mind-Stump	13
5. Sweet and Shiny Distractions	17
6. The First Walk Alone	21
7. The Book That Wrote You	24
8. The Kit Who Wondered Why	27
9. The Ruling Leaf	31
10. Labels That Bind	34
11. Pre-Chosen Winners	37
12. Choosing the Evil	41
13. The Thirteen	46
14. Cloaked in Clause	49
15. Work That Forgets	53
16. The Wall That Welcomes Work	57
17. The River's Toll	61
18. The Hunger That Returns	64
19. The Golden Leash	68
20. Dated and Gated	71
21. Bailouts and Bootouts	75
22. The Shrinking Leaf	78
23. Not Clearly Established	82
24. In-Rem Forfeiture	85
25. The Home You Never Own	88
26. Relief in Disguise	92
27. Crater Day	96
28. The Bittersweet Clinic	101
29. Conditional Freedom	105
30. The Rewriting Mirror	109
31. Recorded Control	113

32. The Bluffed Rungs	117
33. Costly Cure	121
34. Fog of Forms	125
35. Deeds in the Dark	129
36. The Tilted Grove	133
37. Dismissed with Prejudice	137
38. The Pattern-Web	141
39. Fence of Belief	146
40. Two Flocks, One Shear	149
41. The Puppet King	153
42. Beyond the Curtain	157
43. Voice of Flame	162
44. Choosing the Shard	170
45. The Question at the Brink	173
46. Circle of Ears	177
47. Found and Founded	182
48. The Curtain Returns	187
49. The Flame That Listens	192
50. The Answering Silence	195
Epilogue	198
About the Author	201

PROLOGUE
THE CURTAIN AND THE FLAME

They say the Curtain was not made in a day.
It grew from thread, spun to dim the sun's array.
Each beast who touched it felt sheltered and secure,
And then forgot what nature would ensure.

In the heart of the forest where fog hung deep,
Fox awoke from a long, habitual sleep;
Not dreamless, but stirred by a loosening thread
That coiled beneath his paws and snaked in his head.
A murmur kindled like a spark in the breeze,
Then burned in his mind like a blaze in the trees.
A voice from within, a low ember of doubt,
Spoke of the things no one dared to talk about.

'*The world*,' it said to him, '*is woven with care,*
But beauty can trap when it's built to ensnare.
When I vanish, don't trust anything they claim;
Let curiosity crack their sugared game.'

Then on a day when the flame billowed and grew,
His resolve caught fire and his patience withdrew.
The rain began falling, first gentle, then sheer,
And with it began the rise of a new year.
Water on iron, hammered steel kissed with loam,
Like the pulse of the earth, the soul of a home.
Fox let the new scent bring him a hopeful edge,
Yet buried inside lay a path to the ledge.

With questions tightening the cage of his throat,
He prepared to speak, unbound by any quote.
He asked not to scorn, but to slowly reveal,
The truths that were painted, the secrets they'd seal.

Past shows they staged and the edicts they decree,
Will the flame that he follows answer his plea?
Will it blaze when sorrow has swallowed it all?
Will the embers still burn if the Curtain will fall?
Or will it smolder to ash as the daylight climbs high,
And leave him in the silence, wondering why?

Comfort conceals; curiosity reveals.

CHAPTER 1

THE GREAT BEGINNING

Each spring by the bonfire, as blossoms returned,
The forest assembled while vellum was burned.
Ash twisted like glyphs through the lavender air,
And Great Owl's voice rose with theatrical flair.

"In the first breath," said Owl, "there came forth the law:
It fell from the heights and it soothed every flaw.
We were the keepers, the guardians all-wise;
The land was our script to interpret with eyes."
The Owl-Spire kept a warm, algorithmic glow;
Its windows pulsed while circuits processed below.
Smoke curled into code from each page as it burned,
While no one saw the wires beneath what they'd learned.

The goats stood in rows with their heads bowed and grim,
Their teachings split the hush like a hymn grown dim.
The weasels stitched laws with invisible thread,
So keen that the cuts only showed when they bled.

"All life," Owl intoned, "was ordained from the start.
Each creature must follow its heaven-sent part."
The animals nodded, their shoulders drawn tight,
Their fur prickled tense in the anointed light.

"Without us," said Owl, "there'd be peril and pain.
The forest must adapt or order will wane."

But Fox, in the back near an elm wrapped in moss,
Had heard this myth thrice, yet he still felt the loss.
"Who wrote the tale?" he asked. "Who edits the lore?
What truths were erased when they opened that door?"

The crowd fell silent, then Mole lowered his gaze,
And Finch shrank as if she'd heard a banned phrase.
Ringtail leaned in closer from the choir-loft stair:
"They patch it each year. It's a routine repair.
You think it's history? It's only a play.
They doctor the text, then perform the ballet."

As Ringtail remarked, Fox set down his right paw,
A crystal shard bit in and tightened his jaw.
Cold as the first frost and sharper than cut glass,
It clipped him mid-step as he brushed through the grass.

The Great Beginning

A bead of red bloomed where the fur had been cut.
The small wound hurt less than the pain in his gut.
He sensed their '*order*,' so brittle, bright, and prim,
Was a blade that drew blood as it glossed the grim.

"Quiet!" bayed Kinder Goat. "This story is old.
It's sacred, well-tested; its meaning is gold.
We all learn it," she said, her gaze fixed and tight.
"Without its truth, we would be lost in the night.
This tale is our beacon, our root, and our creed;
To question its source is to poison the seed."

"It is never the same," Fox murmured once more.
"Each retelling forgets what the last one swore."

Alpha Wolf fixed him with a glacier-etched stare,
Ears pricked to his doubt like a thorn in the air.

Storm Crow on a branch gave a rough warning cough,
As though dissent's shadow might carry Fox off.

Kit lingered alone with a fern-sheltered rise,
And listened as Fox set a flame to his whys.
Her whiskers gave twitch to a thought left unsaid.
Her mouth nearly spoke, but she stayed still instead.

Her gaze dropped to the wounded paw at his side.
She saw the red nick, and she honored his pride.

The tale rang onward all the way to his bone;
Yet, deep in his marrow, a question had grown:
"What if the beginning," he sighed with a frown,
"Was written to lift only those looking down?"

Start by doubting the start.

CHAPTER 2

KIT AND THE CURTAIN

The forest was tidy, its pathways held straight.
The creatures all marched in a synchronized gait.
Great Owl quoted a scroll from the spire of stone
And sifted which truths might be publicly known.

"The Curtain," he told them, "you must never cross.
It shields your own mind from confusion and loss.
It rose when the woodlands once trembled with flame,
A burden we bear so you're spared from the same."

They nodded in rhythm, aligned in design,
Their concerns were curtailed, then pronounced benign.
Yet Fox's probing words pinched hard at Kit's side,
A pain like a signal the teachers denied.
"What's waiting if I take the Cross-Track ahead?"
She asked, and the elders' expressions turned red.

Sly Weasel bared teeth, fissures in her eyes:
"That question is unsound, and not very wise.

The Curtain is sacred. Don't trouble your mind,
Because disorder begins when norms unwind."

"But who machined its pattern?" she dared to ask,
Her tone low and steady, puncturing the mask.

Writ Vulture replied, "By statute, it is law;
Ratified, sealed, binding upon each paw."
Shade Spider noted it, "Entry logged: dissent."
Her ember eyes filed each motive and intent.

Kit's arm half-lifted, one step toward the light,
But she caught herself, stopped, and stayed in the night.
The pause was brief, yet her focus did not lie.
Her speech was guarded. She needed to know why.

The others just chuckled and nudged her along,
Then mimicked Owl's rules like a nursery song.
Kit blinked at their snickers, her tail pulled in tight,
Ashamed of her questions, though they still felt right.

As the forest anthem rose, paws crossed in time,
Bright voices recited like flags in their prime.
Fat Rat and Grease Boar bargained deals by the fire;
A tusk-tap settled the contract near the choir.

Kit glanced at the Curtain as she held the tune,
Till curiosity swelled just like a balloon.
A ripple ran through it, indistinct and free,
A flaw in the weave no one else seemed to see.

Fox, in the throng, also saw it shift and fade,
And flexed his cut paw where the shard-mark had stayed.
The sting in the skin matched the fault in the air,
But he swallowed his words, too scared to declare.
And in that brief instant, a grave dread would grow,
If any crossed over, he wouldn't dare go.

Fox beheld the Cross-Track, rejoining the crowd,
Though the pulse in his wound beat steady and loud.
The forest moved forward in perfect, clean rows,
While a firestorm burned where Fox's confidence froze.

Look hard; step light.

CHAPTER 3

OWL'S EDICT

Great Owl stood stately on his high spire of stone.
His plumes were burnished with theatrical tone.
His glasses caught starlight, obscuring both eyes,
A specter that dulled each challenge to the wise.

With the anthem finished, Owl's stance posed for show,
He spoke to the forest in measures kept slow.
"The world is as written, no more and no less.
My words are the law meant to steer you through stress.
The forest stays calm when your worries stay few;
Relinquish your burdens, I'll bear them for you."

His voice had a hum like a charm in a snare,
A syrup so sweet it replaced every care.
The public leaned closer, muzzles all aligned,
Their ears tuned to wisdom, their own thoughts resigned.

Fox watched from the rally, his gaze turning dark,
And thumbed at his paw where the shard left its mark.

Owl's Edict

The sting matched the thought that slid into his mind:
What if it's all glass and it breaks from behind?

He raised the same arm as if lifting a stone,
Each tendon resisting the breach of the known.
"How do you know that what's written is law?
Could truth wear a cloak to conceal what we saw?"

Kit watched Fox, his eyes locked, his paw still half-raised,
Memorizing his poise, the way he appraised.
A hunger like foxfire ran lean through her stare,
To learn what he knew and to step where he'd dare.

A hush gripped the ranks; every creature stepped back.
Chill sliced through the air along a knife-thin track.
The stars seemed to blink as the query took hold,
And even the bold felt the evening grow cold.

"Owl is the wisest," said Sly Weasel with pride.
"He's weathered all seasons; he's walked every tide.
You dare to unmake what we've built through the years?
Your dissent fouls up our interlocking gears."

Writ Vulture stalked close with his law-scrolls unfurled,
"Precedent claims doubt will disrupt all our world!"

His talons struck bark where the statutes were scarred:
Shackles meant to keep any questioning barred.

Shade Spider flipped a flag from yellow to red.
Alpha Wolf shadowed routes just one pace ahead.
Neighbors stepped sideways; their welcomes grew too brief.
Fox eyed every exit, aching for relief.

Through latticed boughs, twilight unrolled the sky,
And Owl stood outlined as the lone warding eye.
Fox lowered his gaze and consented, then bowed,
But turned from the perch and slipped out of the crowd.

He wandered that night to the edge of Wild-Grove
And dreamed of a garden, a meadow, a cove,
Where voices painted their own stars in the sky,
And none were commanded to kneel or comply.

Polite tyranny is tyranny.

CHAPTER 4

THE MIND-STUMP

At pale-rose dawn, Fox woke from crown-shadowed dreams,
Where speaking a truth split the night at the seams.
He wandered the paths with his shard-nicked paw sore,
And saw the young ones file to the schoolhouse door.

Inside the Mind-Stump, where the walls thinned to skin,
Young creatures assembled for lessons to begin.
The halls wore portraits of wise owls robed in gold,
With scrolls in their talons and stares diamond-cold.
Kinder Goat with a stick, horn-ringed and well-read,
Taught verses once copied from what the owls said.

"Repeat after me," she uttered sharp and clear:
"Obedience still shields us from doubt and fear.
Be on time. Don't stray. Curiosity sears.
Be grateful for trials, and muffle your ears.
Owls built our great order," she said with a nod,
"And wrote every rule with the blessing of God.

Find joy in the Gold-Leaf that drops from the trees.
We measure your progress. Stay ready to please.
Feelings create trouble," she growled with a glare.
"Poems breed strife. Let no lone verse linger there."

Fawn asked about music; the class rolled their eyes.
"Art serves no purpose," she replied with a rise.
"Freedom is sacrifice, tithe, and toll," she sighed.
"I settle it now, so your minds shall abide."

"What's past the Shield-Mountains?" Kit asked through the green.
"That thinking is rebellious," Goat snapped, eyes keen.
"That's outside the lessons," said Chick, voice unsure.
"They say such notions make your motives impure."

Woodpecker was praised for his dutiful tone,
While Kit drew a scowl for probing the unknown.

The mottos were piped through the moss-scented floor,
As young lungs echoed doctrine the owls once bore.
The walls seemed to breathe with a pulse slow and deep,
A rhythm to rock those awake back to sleep.
They scribbled down rules with reeds sharpened by blade:
Answers prewritten; no question to evade.

The Mind-Stump

Each day in class, Kinder Goat's maxims would stay
In drills that were rehearsed that none could betray.
Some were taught to swallow their very first squeak,
Bred for burrowing, never daring to speak:
Claws bent to sorting, eyes trimmed sharp for charts,
Wings clipped for focus, hearts dimmed into parts.

Bluff Owl at the back wore a grin going thin,
Then blinked when a stray qualm was boxed and fenced in.
"The youth must be built like a well-crafted shoe
To walk through the plains, not wondering what's true."

During break, Kit found a book buried from sight;
A thorn pricked her hide, but it didn't cause blight.
It told of the trees and the truths in the seed,
Of knowledge discovered through hunger and need.

She hid the book from sight with a sidelong glance;
Fox measured the risk in that dangerous chance.
He held back his counsel and would not dissuade,
For dread in his heart said to be not afraid.

That night on a bridge made of riveted steel,
Kit spoke of the teachers who trained what to feel.

She showed Fox the fable, its pages still warm,

And taught of tending that brings gardens their form.

Fox glanced toward the Mind-Stump where owl-lights burned,

And knew it contained facts that would not be learned.

Lesson plans lessen minds.

CHAPTER 5

SWEET AND SHINY DISTRACTIONS

At dawn in the Ear-Hall where gossip was spread,
Possum told Squirrel about the words Fox had said.
"He lifted his paw and asked 'Who wrote the tale,
And who edits and what's kept behind the veil?'"

Sly Weasel heard the murmur, and eyes slid in place.
Possum glanced 'round and saw wolves marked his face.
From rafters, Storm Crow cocked her head at the stir,
And Balm Snake notated her chart for the slur.
Sly Weasel breathed softly to her elite choir,
"Bring sugar and shine; let their questions expire."

Later, Fox was walking the Free-Way through pines,
When a flash split the boughs into dazzling lines.

Storm Crow swooped down laughing, a streak in her beak,
"I've found it!" she cawed. "The treasure we all seek!"

She circled the clearing, letting the crowds increase,
And dangled the glimmer, withholding release.
She dropped it: a pebble, smooth, brilliant, and bright;
It flared like a coal in the green-dappled light.

The animals gasped as their pulses turned slow,
Caught in the gravity of bauble-bright glow.

"It glints!" cried Pearl Magpie. "It leaps into gold.
It brightens my senses. It tightens my hold."
The pebble blazed hotter with fever-dream glare;
Its frost-colored shine locking every last stare.
"But what does it give?" asked Fox, his head inclined.
"A little delight," said Magpie, "for the mind."
Kit gave a quick laugh at the boast she had spun;
Fox caught her smirk and filed it, warm as the sun.

Balm Snake coiled near with a vial at her side,
Lavender mist curling soft, drowsy, and wide.
"Just breathe," came her hiss, "and your burdens will fade
Till your worries dissolve like dew in the glade."

Squirrel's limbs slumped to the ground and then she sighed,
"Life's perfect," she murmured, "no problems inside."

Sweet and Shiny Distractions

Possum shuffled closer, his hammer held low,
But dropped it and the tool landed softly below.
His rafters sagged downward, open to the sky,
His walls left unfinished, the home left to die.

The berry-bins waited, their bottoms laid bare.
The work lay abandoned; no bustle was there.
Fox's chest tightened, both with fear and a spark.
He felt pain in his wound, recalling the dark.

Kit reached for the gem with her widening gaze,
But stopped when she caught Possum lost in a haze.
She frowned at the pebble, stepped back from its pull,
Then edged closer to Fox, her focus now full.
Around them the purple mist climbed through the air,
The sugars consuming what once required care.

Balm Snake half-smiled as eyelids dimmed with the mist;
She logged each creature by name on her list.
Storm Crow preened, delighted, "It does what we say!"
Pearl Magpie glittered, "They will float through the day."
"Too potent," Snake hissed, "they nap, forget the task."
"I will cool the brew, keep paws at work, not ask."

Fox watched the bright trance make the labor go slack.

He banked his small ember and slipped from the track.

He passed through the pines as the dream lost its awe;

Kit watched without speaking and kept what she saw.

Sugar the senses; attention dissolves.

CHAPTER 6

THE FIRST WALK ALONE

The Free-Way was worn by ten thousand before,
Their march well-rehearsed, every shout a set score.
From branches hung edicts in black-inked decree:
'Stand loyal.' 'Walk proudly.' 'Remember you're free.'

Yet under the drone came a note keen and clear;
It rang with a truth over echo and fear.
The sparkle was gone, the recitals felt thin,
And a voice inside said, *Begin from within.*

Fox turned to the Sly-Path where the elms still swayed,
Where no signs were planted and no maps were made.
The moss cooled his stride like a blessing from trees,
As warnings congealed into false-hearted pleas.

He thought of young Kit in the owls' guarded keep,
And her questions that put their facade to sleep.
A warmth rose like embers beneath where he trod,
While the spark in her words defied their false god.

A brook's silver laughter curved low through the wood
And urged him to trek where no cowardice could.
"This road may be bleak," he breathed into the air.
"I'd rather be lost than return to their snare."

The thorns scored his legs with a whip's stinging kiss,
Yet the doubt bit deeper than any of this.
Beyond every ache was a silence with teeth
That gnawed at his heart for the answer beneath.

The ground gave up traces of myths he'd outgrown,
While pieces of comfort were toppled and thrown.
But one lie still lived in the back of his mind,
That walking alone kept the danger confined.

It spared him the lash when the owls cast their blame,
But left him a scar that still carried the shame.
It guarded his body, but fractured his core,
A wound he would bear, more lasting than before.

Somewhere in the dark, past the edges of known,
Is a place without script or a rule-bound tone.
The air felt more honest, though heavy with weight,
And sorrow pressed hard at the threshold of fate.

The First Walk Alone

"I'm afraid," he confessed, "but still I must go.
I don't need the reason; I just need to know."
No banners to follow, no crowd to applaud,
Just questions uncoiled where their certainties clawed.

The journey demanded, its challenge was clear:
Which guide do you follow when no one is near?
He pressed on alone with the strength that he knew,
Hoping to discover a world that is true.

Root in; route out.

CHAPTER 7

THE BOOK THAT WROTE YOU

Fox crept along Sly-Path and entered Peace-Glade,

Where mushrooms grew thick and the morning light strayed.

He didn't yet know which way he was heading,

But purpose would come if he kept on treading.

He stopped by a pond, his anxiety eased,

As birds sang their songs in a green-scented breeze.

He soon came across Key-Cave, swallowed with gloom;

Its vines curled like chains guarding a secret tomb.

One paw pressed the door; it shifted with a sigh,

And it groaned open to where answers would lie.

Within was a hall where the torch-coals burned hot,

And the shelves towered high with the laws long taught.

He drew down a tome rimmed with sinew and dust,

With ink that would neither discolor nor combust.

The Book of Roles bore a subtitle below:

A guide to the natures all creatures must know.

The Book That Wrote You

The pages laid out what each beast had to be.
Their traits boiled down to a simple summary.
He began to read, unsure what he would find.
He froze at an entry that tethered his kind.

"Fox: A sly schemer who deceives through disguise,
Unworthy of trust in society's eyes.
Not fit for decisions, for rule, or command,
They skulk through the margins as others expand."

He flipped through the roles with a growing unease,
As if life were a mask meant only to please.
But near the book's end, where the paper grew thin,
Were pages left blank like a breath held within.

He traced an empty sheet and felt some relief,
As a vision awoke him, unbound by belief:
"Stories, although old, were not fixed in the spine.
The ending is yours; let your paw write the line."

Yet in that blank space, his spirit filled with dread,
He saw Kit in Mind-Stump, confined and misled.
The thought drove his pulse to a hard, rapid beat;
Her flame could be dimmed by a title's deceit.

He closed it, although his distress yet remained,

Though visions kept forming and his chest felt strained.

He returned the tome to where it was first found,

While its dreary contents continued to pound.

If roles can be written, he thought with a cry,

Then who wrote them all and what's the reason why?

Write, or be written.

CHAPTER 8

THE KIT WHO WONDERED WHY

Key-Cave's worry tugged at the back of his mind;
Fox fried oats with corn till the flavors combined.
When breakfast was over, he tidied the stove,
Then merged onto the Free-Way to the Wild-Grove.
He drifted along, weighing what he should do,
And caught a low sob from the shade of a yew.

Kit sat alone while shielding her weepy eyes,
Upset about something and muffling her cries.
"Hey, Kit, are you okay?" Fox called with concern.
"Not really," she sighed with a quiet downturn.
"I left school today. It just didn't feel right."
"Why?" Fox asked gently, his whiskers catching light.

"I've had misgivings," she said, as she stepped near.
"The kind they ignore or pretend not to hear."
He knelt down to meet her inquisitive gaze:
"Not all real challenges are welcomed these days."

"I observed you once," she murmured, softly and slow.
"Asking questions to Kinder Goat and Storm Crow."
He replied, "I glimpsed the Curtain had frayed seams,
And I was told the sight was made by sunbeams."

"I listened to your talk," she feared to admit.
"I hoped to tell you that I also saw it."
"You've seen it?" he pressed. She gave just one small nod.
"I knew at that moment their response was flawed."

They walked for a while with no more words to say,
Then finally voiced what she meant to convey.
"Can I be your student?" she asked with slight shame.
"They call my suspicions a dangerous game.
The elders grow tense when I stop and stare,
Yet I still keep seeing the wires in the air."

Fox probed, "Your parents... do they know you're alone?"
She spoke, "They vanished. I've waited on my own.
Each night at the doorway, I whisper their names;
The porch gives no answer, and the dark hides their flames."

Fox glanced at her heart where her eagerness stirred,
And that old tug returned, too faint to be heard.

Her wonder was sharp, and it pierced through his doubt:
A burden not his that he could not cast out.

He offered no promise, no plan, no decree,
Just room at his side where a student might be.
"Follow, but heed this," he declared with a sigh.
"This road teaches how, not only what or why."

Kit didn't flinch. Instead, she flashed a wide grin.
"I am ready to learn. I want to begin."

He examined her with a pondering gaze,
Not knowing the future of this complex maze.

She brushed past his shoulder, her tail took the lead,
Her pace set by purpose, not matching his speed.
For one breath he paused, with the warning unsaid,
Soon followed her steps where her queries had led.

They walked through the woods where no barriers stood
And forged their own road as they knew that they should.
One worn into silence, the other brand-new,
Both guarding a truth the Curtain couldn't skew.

Like a little candle passed on to a friend,
The spark that was kindled would not ever end.

Then Kit toed a pebble and spoke to the sky,
"I don't want to fight. I just want to know why.
I listen and wonder and try to be fair.
So why is it wrong to ask what waits out there?"

Pupil your pupils.

CHAPTER 9

THE RULING LEAF

Fox and Kit walked the Free-Way where signs hung low,
Past animals queued in a patient, slow row.
"What are you waiting for?" Fox asked Mountain Hare.
"Gold-Leaves for our labor are provided there."

They followed the line to a hill steep and wide,
Where badgers in cloaks stitched with gold-threaded pride.
The Mint-Tree behind them, stone trunk, branches brass,
Clicked out currency from behind the thick glass.

Fox stepped with Kit up to the badger-run stand.
"What are these?" she asked, trying to understand.
"You earn them," said Mint Badger, "through toil and strain.
Creatures can dig, drag, or harvest the grain."

"And then," said Caribou, "we trade them for bread.
Without them, we starve or go roofless instead."
Kit studied the ground. "But who sets the amount?
And who holds the keys to this sacred account?"

Mint Badger replied, "We determine what's paid.
Leaves steady the market; they're better for trade.
Money is distributed, counted, and signed,
And the system was sealed as wisely designed."

Meanwhile, Bronze Badger worked the line with a frown;
She smoothed it away as the next one came down.

Fox caught that small crease, but it vanished too fast,
An inkling of doubt: perhaps she would not last.

"What if the fixed value," Fox asked, "is pretend,
Like stories the goats twist, revise, and defend?"
"It works," said Mint Badger. "It's steady and fair.
The owls forged the process with diligent care."

At dusk, while the forest lay hushed and asleep,
Fox led Kit back with a shiver that ran deep.
They entered the concourse, cloaked under the eaves,
Where gilders pressed symbols on each of the Leaves.

They piled them in strongboxes, locked them away,
Releasing mere crumbs on the following day.
Kit's focus narrowed. "They mint more than they give."
"They control," Fox said, "so they choose who can live."

The Ruling Leaf

He glared at the bank with suspicion laid bare,
Then muttered, "A myth backed by nothing but air."

"Stay hidden," Fox whispered, "I'll slip in by stealth."
She watched him creep toward the crates of their wealth.
From shadow, he lifted a sheaf from a chest,
And felt how their worth sat false within his vest.

Slate Wolf smelled a stranger and circled the stacks;
Her pawprints, like commas, hunted down the tracks.
Fox staggered a false trail with torn moss and bark,
And slipped back to Kit to flee into the dark.

That night he dreamt of the pebble in the glade,
And sweet mist loomed while the fruit slowly decayed.

Leaves leave hunger.

CHAPTER 10

LABELS THAT BIND

Dawn shook the last shiver from his fevered dreams.
Kit was gone, so Fox began normal regimes.
His breakfast was scant, just a heel he could spare,
And he followed the Free-Way to the Trade-Square.

Then he paused by a stump where Kit sat alone;
Her whiskers pulled tight, her voice barely a tone.
"I spoke about how Gold-Leaves are made each day,"
She murmured, "and Chicken just laughed it away."

"She flared up and clucked, 'That's the danger of doubt!'
And called me a menace for speaking straight out.
She said I sow trouble; I stir and I shame.
For one simple statement, I'm called a bad name."

Fox lowered himself calmly next to her side,
His voice dark with heat he refused to let slide.
"They twist every word into thorns that will sting
And bind them to names, a punishable thing.

Labels That Bind

'*Order,*' they say, as if insight will decay.
'*Traitor,*' to snuff out what you meant to convey.
Words like '*unsafe,*' '*unreal,*' and simply '*too new*':
They silence the question, not answer what's true."

Kit's ears flickered once. "But they sound so polite."
"That's the point," Fox replied, "to make wrong feel trite.
They keep truths in disguise and believe the lies,
That closes the mind while it brightens their eyes.
They'll wield stability to stall what's begun
And honor to armor the harm that they've done.
'*Tradition,*' '*respect,*' '*be cordial,*' '*know your place,*'
They sculpt us to fit in an elegant space.
The goats call it '*virtue,*' the owls call it '*peace,*'
But each phrase is chosen to make your thoughts cease.
The weasels repeat it until it sounds right,
And label you if you continue to fight."

They rose from the stump as the dawn took the lane,
And her spirits lifted like grass after rain.
From Rush-River beyond came a scent that was clear,
And Kit felt better, but her eyes still showed fear.

For a heartbeat the tightness in Fox was eased,
Then anxiety returned and swiftly squeezed.

His tail-tip trembled. The forest grew too near;
The label scribed for Kit echoed in his ear.

She noticed. She placed a paw on his forearm,
No speech, only comfort: no need for alarm.
Fox breathed the reed-sweet river into his chest,
And held to that joy till the dread came to rest.

They walked on in silence, the water behind,
Its silver glow folding the dark into kind.

Label the labeler.

CHAPTER 11

PRE-CHOSEN WINNERS

They took the Free-Way toward the Trade-Square bend,
But found a fresh signpost hammered at the end.
A board of green-gilt letters caught them off guard,
'*LEAF-SQUARE*,' it read, rebranding the old courtyard.

With chalk and twine, Arch Beaver defined the lines
To build a stage to suit the Thirteen's designs.
Dock Rat barked out orders to a hustling crew,
While nails pounded the wood as new structures grew.

The creatures stared in the middle of the churn.
Rove Goat stood tall, horns marked by what we all earn.
The scrolls were unfurled as he read out the verse:
"Those born in the canopy live without curse.
Those from the roots must contribute and remain.
Balance demands that we all stay in our lane."

Fox listened from the back, his breath held like thread,
Kit low at his flank, ears trained on what was said.

The words carried lessons like sap through the breeze,
Bending the public's minds till they felt at ease.

Gilt Magpie swept in with a sash made of rings.
He sparkled like frost and displayed many things.
"I carry the weight of the dreams I fulfilled.
These baubles were earned by lands my father tilled."

Storm Crow by the Ear-Hall wrote down every phrase:
"A quote for the papers to inspire our days."
Wren cried out, "But we also worked to ascend!
My father digs and there's no food at the end!"

Rove Goat only nodded. "Mine deeper, he must.
The worthy rise upward. The fallen are dust."
But when Magpie drew near, Goat's eyes slid aside;
His jaw gave a slight tic he could not quite hide.

Fox saw that small tremor and filed it away,
A crack in the wood that might splinter someday.
Kit saw him observing and caught his intent,
Learning the aspects of the signs of dissent.
She watched how his gaze mapped the smallest of breaks;
How roots stay firm when the surface faintly shakes.

Gilt Magpie dropped morsels from gem-coated plates,
Feeling remorse for the poor creatures' fates.
When Wren reached for crumbs, he was stopped by a claw,
His hope split apart by the edge of that law.

Near the fruit stand, Possum sat low in the weeds
Chewing a carrot stem to muffle his needs.
Kit glanced once his way. He offered a shrug.
"They teach us the rules, but they don't fill the jug."

Rove Goat shut his ledgers, then Wren bowed his head;
His feathers turned dull from the doctrines they fed.
While no one was looking, he tucked in his cheek,
A seed he had pilfered, a truth yet to speak.

Fox's chest warmed at that deceptive display,
The sense to hide food when hunger became prey.

He stepped from the mob, but Rove Goat met his stare:
"The stream has its channels. Your course flows elsewhere."
Fox asked, "And who carved this truth into the bark?"
"The forest," Goat answered. "Its wisdom is stark."

Magpie spun once on his platinum-capped toe,
His laughter a chime with a venomous flow.

"If questions could crown you, then where is your throne?
Success sings the song, so you earn what you own."

Gilt Magpie flew off with his shadow spread wide,
And the rest were told softly, "Swallow your pride."
Fox murmured to Kit as they slipped from the site,
"They plant us and then grade our growth in their light."
And Wren, in the crowd, kept the kernel concealed
To tuck in the earth when the furrows had healed.

Gilt gilds guilt.

CHAPTER 12

CHOOSING THE EVIL

At dawn they woke inside the den of red clay,
Then took the Free-Way back to Leaf-Square's array.
Fox had brought Gold-Leaves with reluctance and pain,
Cash only, no barter, made trading in vain.

Fox and Kit wandered, food baskets in tow,
Past traders still stacking up produce and dough.
They'd come for the herbs they had planned to collect,
But found only pamphlets on whom to elect.

A sign swayed above in the courtyard's warm air:
Election Now Open! All voices prepare.

The yard had been staged with flamboyant motifs,
Vote for a candidate that fits your beliefs.
Gold-inked slogans shimmered from bunting and board:
A Thriving Future! in script all beasts adored.

Below were three posters, slick smiles and neat fur,
Each spouting old phrases with polished new purr.

The weasels gave speeches with well-practiced air,
Though none had ever stepped forth to help or care.
And high in the spire, behind a concealed screen,
Great Owl tweaked the wires of the stage-run routine.

One barked about safety, the next about pride,
The last vowed more grain, yet the bins gaped inside.
"They're different!" cried Dove. "Hear the words they speak!
Each path moves us forward; no hoof leaves the weak!"

Fox studied the names, each rehearsed honeyed line.
They wore matching medals, the same subtle sign.
"Can others run, too?" he asked, Anteater near.
The beast's brow pinched tight. "That's not how it works here.
The elders decide who is purest and clean."
Kit read through the options, her gaze turning keen.

Cardinal passed, clutching his purse to his chest,
And whispered, "The wolves said this choice is the best."
Kit marked his allegiance, his bias to Sly.
She shelved that for later, to pull and apply.

Choosing the Evil

Goats guarded the booths in their scholar-cut coats,
Reciting the rules in precise, sacred notes.
"Your duty is sanctioned," they bleated with pride,
"To vote is to honor the law we abide."

"Participation," Rove Goat rigidly said,
"Proves wisdom prevails in the path we all tread."
Fox stepped to a stand, but his paw gave a sting,
The shard-cut from spring now a faint, tender ring.

He lifted the stylus to mark down his slate.
Kit gently stayed his claw, "Don't leave this to fate.
Grass Weasel sounds so brave. Do not make such haste.
She holds your heart, but your vote would be a waste.
Wolves back Sly Weasel, installed in the top seat.
So choose Masked Weasel to hasten Sly's defeat."

"Three weasels," said Fox, "in the same painted mask.
They trade out the colors and keep to one task.
They dance different steps, yet answer one lord,
Then bow to the donors who fatten their hoard."
He folded his ballot and left it unsigned,
And walked past the urn with his jaw set, resigned.

Fox did not cast a vote, but stood where winds twist.
His words struck the air like a match in the mist.
Kit snapped, "You abstained. You surrendered your say.
Now keep your complaints and your grumbles at bay."

Fox answered, "If you choose thieves, then bear the blame.
You have hired the harm. Its ruin wears your name.
Their damage is yours: you stamped it with your choice.
You lent them your trust and traded out your voice.
I cast nothing at all. My conscience stays free,
So I keep my right to denounce what I see."

Kit's ears went back, but she turned toward the crowd;
The booth drew her regard, its curtains a shroud.
The ballots were locked in a brass-plated crate,
Then hauled to the vault for the clerks to collate.

The beasts swarmed the square for the counting day show,
Unaware the outcome was fixed long ago.
And votes, though totaled, were shaped to a set plan.
The results were devised before it began.

Fox paid for dry roots and turned back on the track.
The Free-Way led home with the dusk at his back.

Choosing the Evil

The tally bell rang: Sly Weasel took the crown.

Kit muttered, "Your silence just carried it down."

Fox said, "Evil is still evil. Call the lie.

Choose "lesser evil,: and still you wear the tie."

Polled by many; pulled by money.

CHAPTER 13

THE THIRTEEN

A week since the tally, the banners hung dry;
They walked at sunset while the lamps met the sky.
Kit's anger had cooled like a coal under ash;
She matched him in silence, no need for a clash.

An aroma rode the wind, homely and slow,
Of berries and honey and mushrooms aglow.
Fox inhaled the warm scents with Kit close behind,
Hunger pulling thought from the back of his mind.

The creatures lay quiet on burlap and thread.
Their bellies collapsed, their eyes rimmed with red.
"That smell," sighed Raccoon, his voice brittle and creased,
"Is dinner at Grand-Keep where the elite feast."

Up past the undergrowth, the High-Fence would rise,
Its gold-spined thorns sharp under watchful wolf eyes.
There stood a castle with an ivory crown:
Its ovens blazed hot while the poor gathered down.

The Thirteen

Fox scaled a cedar and edged through the thin screen,
To spy thirteen beasts at a gold-heaped cuisine.

Great Owl, smoke-gray, set the story's guiding track.
Alpha Wolf, snow-white, kept ranks tight in his pack.
Mint Badger added ledgers with coin-bright claws.
Writ Vulture signed orders to legalize flaws.

Arch Beaver set seating by blueprints and stone.
Grease Boar split the haunch till it gleamed to the bone.
Pearl Magpie arrayed all the plates into rows.
Storm Crow cued the news; she choreographed shows.

Balm Snake poured a cordial of milky-green sweet.
Kinder Goat penned lessons on her chalk-scratched sheet.
Fat Rat licked the gravy and counted the rake,
While Sly Weasel slid papers for each beast's stake.

Shade Spider drew patterns as lanterns went dim.
Dark shadows enclosed the banquet's farthest rim.

Fox's toes sank deep as the truth burned his chest:
"It's not that there's nothing; it's fenced and possessed."
He slid through a service gap under the eaves,
And palmed a honey flatbread wrapped in fig leaves.

Slate Wolf's kinked tail pricked. Her sharp nails dug in scree.

She knew that same spoor from his raid at Mint-Tree.

Fox slipped past the guard and dropped the bread below.

Kit tucked it and hid it where sentries won't know.

Back in the dark forest, they broke it apart:

Warm crumbs, seeded-sweet, like a pulse in the heart.

Wolves hunted near as the bodies pressed all tight.

The crowd shifted slowly to block Kit from sight.

An eye-flick to Ringtail, a paw-tilt to Doe,

They passed pieces along to where they should go.

One pressed the last morsel into Fox's paw:

A trust between them where the famine was law.

Kit mirrored the signal, her chin lifted high:

A small leader's spark in the frost-bitten sky.

Fox watched her, uneasy, yet warmed by the grace.

The cloaked rebellion sparked to life in this place.

What the Keep keeps, the Keep eats.

CHAPTER 14

CLOAKED IN CLAUSE

Kit walked to the Mind-Stump at first light of day,
To find her friend Pup after seasons away.
Pup laughed, "You came back! I had feared you were gone."
He waved her to join as the morning moved on.

They passed by a poster nailed firm to the wall,
THE EQUITY ACT: JUSTICE AND GOOD FOR ALL.
But small printed lines twisted fair into fraud,
And Kit felt a chill as she silently awed.

She couldn't explain what was wrong in the phrase,
But something rang false in sugared, gilded praise.
"It sounds fair, but not equality," she said,
And hurried to Fox with the thought in her head.

His shard-cut paw pulsed, a sharp, remembered dread,
But her eyes held the truth: denial was dead.
"Equality keeps one measure for each case,
While equity allots by caste and by place.

All right," said Fox, "we'll watch them debate the bill."
They trekked for the Leaf-Dome on Capitol-Hill.

Its gold-veined stained glass crowned the mountain's cold pride,
Masking the hands that crafted the deals inside.
Fox sat in the bleachers with Kit by his knee
To watch the matter unfold for all to see.

Hedge Boar came bristling, burrs still in her hide.
Tree sap glazed her tusks; old scars tugged at her stride.
In polished boots, she set a satchel of pay
And muttered, "Just file this the usual way."

Bronze Badger stepped in, her brow-band copper-bright;
Her penny-dulled nails caught the dust in the light.
She tallied the coins, a pause between Gold-Leaves,
And inked a footnote no honest beast believes.

Plea Vulture, dusk-rose, with her ruff worn to fray,
Kept both wings tucked close, her gaze sliding away.
She drafted the details, scanned clauses: "*all fine*,"
Called it "*sound*," yet her beak lingered on each line.

From the floor rose Sly Weasel with a stern stare,
"To keep the land free, we must all do our share."

Cloaked in Clause

Yet hidden below was a bypass they slipped;
It lifted their friends while the others were clipped.
She spoke of fairness and of the public cause,
And bowed to her donors with velveted claws.

Sly Weasel paused with a paper sealed in wax,
And whispered to Boar, "Here is your loophole tax."
Rat pages slid plates heavy-laden with bread,
On fruits from a table, the taxpayers' spread.

Dock Rat, lean and matted, tar-smeared from the pier,
A rope-burn on her tail, one toe lost last year.
She jotted her notes on the clause and the law,
Then nodded to Hedge Boar, yet tasting the flaw.

Their placards declared, *All opinions shall weigh*,
But Fox saw the outcome already in play.
No voices were raised. Proceedings simply sped.
The bill had been passed before minutes were read.

Kit whispered, "They vote to ratify what's set.
The totals were fixed before committees met."
The hum of the Dome pressed down on her soul,
"I'm only a passenger, not in control."

Applause sealed the chamber; footnotes set the rate.

They sold it as balance and named it as fate.

They bill for audits, trainings, badges, and seals,

And sell the scoring that rations out meals.

But the Act didn't help creatures become free;

It tethered their time to a debt they can't see.

Clause for them; claws for us.

CHAPTER 15

WORK THAT FORGETS

Weeks slid since the Act, like frost seeping in clay:
No trumpet of change, just a slow drift each day.
A rumor had spread of a mill leaking ooze,
So they left the den to go confirm the news.
Fox and Kit hiked the Free-Way, eyes open wide;
Where gardens once fed, now billboards would preside.

New placards leaned crooked along the day's road,
Equity earns care, a bold slogan bestowed.
Insurance through employment, the footnote warned.
Fox traced the fine script and felt quietly scorned.

They passed the Mind-Stump to a foul-smelling hill,
Where a new factory stood called the Sweet-Mill.
The air clawed their nostrils, so bitter with rust,
Old iron on their tongues, blood-salt and brown dust.
Fox and Kit walked the lanes of girders and wheels,
Past fumes, long conveyors, and padlocked bay seals.

They saw Turkey sewing a blue and white flag,
His shoulders were slumping, his feathers all sag.
"What's it for?" Fox inquired, his voice soft and low.
Turkey grunted dull, "I don't exactly know.
I think it's for a conflict. I forgot which.
We're always at war, and the foes tend to switch."

Chipmunk processed acorns for reasons unknown.
The shells were discarded, and none were her own.
"They say it's important," she muttered with dread,
"But I never eat them. I'm paid Leaves instead."

Dock Rat with a clipboard walked brisk through the field
And moaned when Chipmunk's productivity reeled.
"Efficiency's down," she warned with a click,
Then stalled at Chipmunk's name; her heartbeat grew quick.
Her claw held the form, though her posture was slack.
She stiffened again, and the rhythm came back.
She uttered the metric through clenched, weary teeth,
"We need to let you go if you fall beneath."

Kit kept her eyes fixed on the cadence and pace;
Her lips shaped the words, a blank mask on her face.
Soon her ears snapped rigid, her whiskers drew tight,
Before she turned abruptly and slipped from sight.

Fox quickly followed Kit to a stream that slowed;
Where the creek once sang, pollution now flowed.

Otter lay mourning on a dock in the sun,
"I was paid until the water couldn't run.
I am no longer able to earn my keep,
And the only thing I now can do is weep."

They passed an office where black charts lined the wall.
Badgers tracked items to be billed to them all.
A notice hung centered: *EQUITY. FAIR SHARE*,
Tick-marks like teeth penned in the Sweet-Mill's smoked air.

"Sugar boosts their mood," said Fat Rat with a grin,
"Candy helps keep their metrics humming within."

"This craft," Fox muttered, "once produced something more,
But it merely provides what sells in a store."
"They track their minutes," Kit said, "not what they make."
"The Act bought their time," he sighed, "and forged the ache."
The lesson hit hard in the mill's pounding din:
Work stripped of its meaning leaves nothing within.

He felt the gray settle like ash on his chest;
The clang and the ledgers permitted no rest.

The creek tasted coins, even sunlight seemed sold;
And every soft heartbeat got tallied and tolled.

As afternoon softened beneath the broad trees,
They came to a hedgerow alive with the bees.
They labored for nectar and danced through the day:
No bells, no orders, only blossoms and play.

Kit watched how the clock ate the marrow of noon,
And knew how a life can be traded too soon.
"Keep love for your craft," she said, "not price-tagged worth.
Choose work that binds you to wind, water, and earth."

Make time for life; not life for time.

CHAPTER 16

THE WALL THAT WELCOMES WORK

At daybreak they went to Leaf-Square to buy bread.
The Sweet-Mill's gray smoke still hung like bitter spread.
Storm Crow raised placards: *Congress: public debate.*
Purity Act is heard today. Don't be late!

Kit met Fox's glance: "I think we should be there."
He nodded once: "Yes. We'll watch the whole affair."

They then took to the Free-Way at a brisk stride,
To where Knot-Hall and the Leaf-Dome both collide.

Inside, Sly Weasel addressed the crowded hall,
"Our forest is pure. Outsiders? Ban them all!
They bring us diseases, their customs unclean,
Their burrows breed rot in the heart of our green."

Writ Vulture wrote "safe harbor" into code now.
Rats filed self-audits. Wolves let them slide somehow.

Beavers would build the walls and checkpoints for show;
But arrests hit workers, not bosses they know.

Applause rose and rang in the chamber's gold pane,
While Fox felt a headache arise in his brain.
They departed and followed the carts downhill,
Past mint-colored posters for *Order* and *Will*.

They entered the Shade-Slums where few treetops grew
And observed the Tall-Wall with its black-steel hue.
The sign at its base ordered, *Be proud. Stand guard*.
Those bold-faced letters made giving aid seem hard.

Tamarin sat down near a rundown estate
With rope burns on her hands, her ribs sharp as slate.

She whispered in gasps, "I no steal... only trade.
I sweat in the sun till my body is frayed."

Fox crouched: "Who hired you from the border Cross-Gate?"
She murmured, "Crew boss runs through checkpoints, as freight.
We dig near Rush-River, then vanish from sight.
No name. No permiso. We drudge through the night."

The Wall That Welcomes Work

Fox asked, "What's built upriver? What is the plan?"
She answered, "They just say to dig all you can.
We load in the darkness. We break. We descend.
We don't get to know what it is in the end.
They pay us in chits to sleep in this borough,
Then housing and permits keep our income low.
Rat boss keeps our Leaves till the season is through,
And if we complain, we are told, '*Who are you?*'"

An unmarked flatbed rumbled up, braking slow.
Fat Rat checked his list and called numbers by row.
"Crew seven, line up. Wristbands out for the scan."
Tamarin tucked backwards and shrank from the van.

Alpha Wolf strolled by with a paper and pen.
Fox and Kit withdrew behind the run-down den.
Wolf scented the air, then continued on past.
The cart coughed twice and began rolling at last.

They followed the flatbed along fresh-cut roads,
Where homes rose quickly on the cheapest of loads.
At dusk, crews were gone, all the carts rolled away.
By dark, *NO TRESPASSING* signs were on display.

THE FOX WHO WONDERED WHY

Fox stared at new homes till his world narrowed thin.
Kit gripped his forearm, "This is where we begin."
She warmed their day's bread in the cup of her palm,
Then passed half of it to him, quiet and calm.

Steel the wall; steal the labor.

CHAPTER 17

THE RIVER'S TOLL

At dawn, Tamarin's warning tugged like a thread
Of work on Rush-River where night crews were led.
Two swallows of broth, a crust to clear the head.
Kit quenched the wick: "Let's check the rumor," she said.

Fox trailed the Sly-Path where Rush-River ran dry,
Through sun-brittled reeds under dragonfly sky.
Kit shadowed his footfalls, her questions in tow;
Where rapids once argued, now bedrock lay low.

The air tasted hollow, the stones held a trace,
Of the living current that graced this razed place.
At last, near the cliffs where the valley grew steep,
They saw how the river was chained in the deep.

It clattered, not flowed, in a stammering stall,
Held back by a barrier, rigid and tall.
A sign in bold black letters, *RUSH-DAM* declared,
While beavers ensured not a fracture was spared.

The locks opened in sequence, pipes hissed with steam;
Badgers set tariffs for every rationed stream.
Notice signs in black ink warned all beasts *Beware:*
To keep us from ruin, we all do our share.
Each brick was planted with meticulous pride;
Laws drafted by hand so the dam could abide.

High on a ledge, in a turret made of glass,
Masked Weasel decreed that slow water should pass.
"Rush-Dam gives light for schools and the winter night.
Your dens will stay warm; this bargain keeps us right.
We give up some flow, a prudent, modern way.
A meager concession," he chose to relay.

They left the cold dam and made for the Leaf-Square
To audit the lies that were sold off as care.
Below, in the courtyard, the creatures held jars,
Begging for swallows through the welded-shut bars.
Rush-River, once wild from the mountain to glade,
Now trickled through ledgers Mint Badger had made.

Cardinal stumbled in line, clutching his cup,
His beak chipped and empty, his pinions drawn up.
"I have a large savings from working last year,"
He whispered, low, to Kit, so no wolves could hear.

The River's Toll

"Now I pay for these drops that once ran untolled;
They levy a tariff, yet it feels we were sold."

Fox turned from the crowd, his teeth set hard in strain.
What once poured freely had been measured for gain.
Frog reached out for the spout, her lips cracked and dry;
Too desperate to pause, too poor to comply.
A wolf yanked her backward; her jar hit the stone,
Then burst into clatter: the mouthfuls were thrown.
Fox winced at the sound; it echoed in his ears,
A ringing he carried for many more years.

Kit knelt at a rivulet threading the slate;
Then cupped it in silence, her stance set with weight.
"Follow the money," she uttered without fear,
"I see it," replied Fox, "and the theft is clear.
They metered the water. They marked the vale sold.
The commons were tallied and totaled in gold."

From free flow to fee flow.

CHAPTER 18

THE HUNGER THAT RETURNS

Fox headed for Wild-Grove with Kit keeping pace;
They passed the Sweet-Mill with its cloying embrace.
Its chimneys coughed ribbons through cracks in the trees,
Aromas that curled with the late-summer breeze.
The berries were gone. The beets slept under clay.
Yet every last nest claimed they feasted each day.
The wrappers blew wild through the dirt and the pine,
Lurid scraps that fluttered like flags of decline.

Fox blinked in surprise as Chickadee passed twice,
Still chewing a cake that smelled lovely with spice.
Its glaze made her feathers gleam yellow and red,
But something felt wrong in the bob of her head.

They followed the scent trail to a rat-run tent,
Where platters were stacked and the labels were bent.
Ink Crow squawked, "Only two Gold-Leaves for a bite!
They're packed with the sun and make your tail feel light!"

The Hunger That Returns

He smudged at his badge till the print lost its wink.
He weighed his words, then let his sales talk sink.

The queue stretched around through the ash and the loam,
Where Eastern Cottontail took boxes back home.
Inside was candy with translucent blue skin,
That fizzed as they broke and ran thick down the chin.
Gecko grew rounder with each slow-buzzing chew,
Then he stumbled and wheezed as his lungs withdrew.

Scrub Snake in a white lab coat proclaimed with pride,
"Each product was inspected and verified.
Enjoy without worry; there's nothing to fear.
Our findings are sound, and the science is clear."
His gaze fell to Kit. His cadence lost its will.
He checked the clipboard. The meaning wavered still.

Fox stared at the bags in the back of the stall.
Inside, the mix wriggled and hissed by the wall.
Each bore a sticker from the Council of Health,
With words like *Wholesome!* and *For the Commonwealth*.

Fox sniffed at a bun that a stag left behind.
It fizzled and sparked with a sweetness refined.

THE FOX WHO WONDERED WHY

He nudged it aside with the tip of his toe,
But noticed his belly still rumbled below.

Kit whiffed at the frosting, its smell honey-kissed,
"It reminds me of the pebble and sweet mist."
She pushed back the roll with its glittery coat,
"This leaves something sharp, like a thorn in my throat."

Soon Plea Vulture swept down from a rocky perch,
And tacked up a bulletin outside the church.
"If sickness should rise from these powders or pies,
All claims are denied and we cannot advise."

Puma complained because her cub couldn't run.
Plea Vulture replied, "There's no proven harm done.
But parents like you should limit what you feed;
His symptoms don't prove there's a problem, indeed."
Her words echoed back, and she heard what she said.
For one quiet heartbeat, the certainty fled.

At dusk, they saw piles of fur near the dry creek,
Too bloated to move and too sluggish to speak.

The more they consume, the hungrier they feel:
Each wrapper a lure for a lab-crafted meal.

The Hunger That Returns

The sky changed its color, the silence was vast,
And still the plastic sleeves refused to burn fast.

Kit watched Puma's cub plead for a little more.
"They cannot stop feeding on what's at the store."
"This isn't healthy," she said. "It's like a chain."
Fox asked, "If this makes them sick, who gains from pain?"

Eat processed; be processed.

CHAPTER 19

THE GOLDEN LEASH

After Rush-Dam invoiced coins for the water,
And Sweet-Mill sold food that makes creatures totter,
Leaf-Square raised a booth with *Relief* cast in gold.
Kit tugged Fox to hear what the scribes had foretold.

They continued to tread lightly through the square,
Past beasts in a queue with their hunger laid bare.
Mint Badger announced with his velveteen charm,
"We are here to help. There's no cause for alarm.
Take ten golden notes, you don't need to repay,
Until later, of course, on some future day."

Paws reached for the pens with solace in their eyes,
But the ink on each scroll was a coiled disguise:
"*For every Leaf borrowed, you must pay back two,
With interest daily for services due.
If payment falls short, we will foreclose your den,
Then we may rent it to someone else again.*"

The Golden Leash

At the edge of the stalls stood Otter alone,
With her whiskers taut-drawn, her stance hard as stone.
"They say I don't qualify, due to my job,
But I've patched my home the best I can with cob."

Bronze Badger smiled and said, "Too risky to lend.
This rate is our lowest. I wish I could bend."

Fox scanned the loan terms and his stomach dropped low,
The numbers would triple before she could know.
And in that moment, he saw Kit years ahead,
Signing her life away to sleep in a bed.
The ground dropped underfoot: his knees almost gave.
Her paw took his weight. She would not let him cave.

After three months, they revisited Leaf-Square.
The lines snaked the cobbles; the stalls were half bare.

Shrew, once content, now dug his holes not for fun,
But eight hard hours a day under the sun.
His spine had gone crooked, his voice rough with debt,
And Mint Badger reminded, "You owe us yet."

Hawk had plucked her feathers to settle her loan.
Her wings hung wilted, stripped to the naked bone.

Grounded by credit, she had lost all her flight,
A hunter once feared, now was robbed of her might.

The owls called it "fairness"; the vultures kept score,
Badgers cooed "kindness" while tightening much more.

"The Leaf sticks like a thorn," Fox growled with a frown.
"It's bait on a hook that will drag the soul down.
You pay debts with work and time becomes a fee.
Each borrowed tomorrow buys chains you can't see."

Kit said, "They sign blind to the prices they'll pay.
They just hope to keep afloat another day."
Fox narrowed his gaze, "It's a deceiver's game.
But who keeps them owing while fanning the flame?

Credit credits the creditor.

CHAPTER 20

DATED AND GATED

A new day unlatched with a soft river-spray.
They shunned Leaf-Square's booths and went hunting today,
For mushrooms and thickets of ripe blueberries.
No premade loaves; instead, they chased wild cherries.

They took the Sly-Path, keeping close to the edge,
Past Rush-Dam's high buttress, stone shoulder, and ledge.
The reservoir rising has covered the trail;
The footway now sleeps under the water's veil.
So hugging the beachline, they kept to the shore;
They paced by the driftwood, eyes reading the floor.

They at last reached Wild-Grove, where cool breezes blew,
And were stopped at entry, barred from going through.
They backed from the fence, instincts tugging with dread.
Slate Wolf stood guard under a notice that read:
DO NOT ENTER: GROVE UNDER SEASONAL REST
(Unless you are an invited, listed guest).

Pearl Magpie slipped in with carts of empty crates.
Fat Rat rolled a Sweet-Mill cart marked *Special Rates*.
Oriole came hopeful with clean-circled jars;
Slate Wolf lifted up the plank and raised the bars.
Oriole stepped back from the iron-braced gate,
The crossbar held fast; he'd simply come too late.

Fox tipped Kit to bracken behind the large stone.
They lay like flat shadows and watched plans be sown.
Masked Weasel stepped in with the rope-rolled law scroll.
Grease Boar and Arch Beaver marked maps to control.

"Leaf-Dome will pass it," Weasel murmured, "but see,
You've got it before they do; your profit's free."
Wild-Grove rests today; we keep pickers away.
Next month Open-Range shuts; grains are kept at bay.
Orchard-Belt stays open per the posted dates,
Then closes as tamarins move through the gates."

Grease Boar palmed the list with a ledger-slick smile,
"Night crews will harvest. Keep the latch shut meanwhile."
Masked Weasel looked down. "These closures guard the trees."
Grease Boar snorted, "The scarcity pays the fees."

Pearl Magpie flashed her Gold-Leaves: "I'll bankroll this,
And rebrand it *Wild-Grove Rare* to sell as bliss."
Fat Rat pressed the labels on sugar-bright tin,
"Triple the profit," he squeaked, "and we all win."

Arch Beaver marked posts on a long, folded chart,
"I'll raise the Free-Range's fence to do my part.
Then log soil tests later; upgrades may start here."
Grease Boar nodded; his smile grew from ear to ear.

Slate Wolf raised her muzzle and tasted the air,
"Mint-Tree... Grand-Keep... thief..." and a new odor there.
Fox whispered, "Let's move now. The wind blow our scent,
And use the waterway to hide where we went."

A flock of gulls kicked up a whitening breeze;
Slate Wolf checked the rustle among the tall trees.
She tested the wind line, tracing every turn,
Found damp, splayed footprints; she logged what she could learn.
She combed through the shrubs, but nothing was there now.
She filed two odors and returned to her vow.

They waited until no more footfalls drew near.
The silence grew steady; their pathway was clear.

"So the secret," said Kit, "is the closing date?"
"Yes," Fox said. "Know first, then sell at a high rate.
When law picks the window and fewer are told,
Their chosen dates now turn hunger to gold."

They turned toward Leaf-Square, with baskets still bare,
And paid for the food the Wild-Grove wouldn't share.

Date the gate; rate the take.

CHAPTER 21

BAILOUTS AND BOOTOUTS

At dawn, Fox and Kit took to the market road,
Past "Relief" loan posters that tallied what's owed.
Fox paused at the due-cards, nailed stiff, stamped in ink,
As Kit watched the borrowers' hopes start to sink.

The food stands had twisted, roots torn in a flood,
And fear seeped through the forest's unstable blood.
Gold-Leaves vanished from banks quickly overnight,
And panic spread as frost in the failing light.

Fox stood in Leaf-Square where the trading once sang;
Beside him, Kit watched as no morning bell rang.
Merchants packed empty crates that were lined with dust,
And the air held its breath, heavy with distrust.

From the rim, they saw Sly Weasel take the stage:
"We must act at once, or collapse will engage.
Support must be swift, though mistakes have been made,
Or the trade we need will begin to degrade."

Writ Vulture swept in with a stack of decrees,
"Some took on too much, but they did so with ease.
The risk was assumed with full legal accord,
But losses are a public case," he deplored.

Great Owl praised the fix from his ivory spire,
Then rats hiked up the costs to stoke the empire.
The elites grew fatter, their ledgers reborn,
And the creatures' houses were trampled and torn.

Grease Boar hauled a crate stamped *EMERGENCY AID*,
And skimmed off a cut in a shadow he'd laid.
The badgers booked windfalls, their ledgers restored,
As bailouts ran upward while foreclosures soared.

Starling, who stitched linens for nobles in flight,
Lost her employment by the end of the night.
In the raw dawnlight, her company was gone;
The economy crashed, her savings withdrawn.

Fox looked at Starling in the harsh, settling chill;
Her feathers were dulled, and her posture was still.
Her voice, a shard of glass, pricked deep through the gloom,
"My home will be foreclosed. Now I face my doom."

Bailouts and Bootouts

Kit felt an ember, a fire under flintstones,
A burn she ignored but could feel in her bones.
No claws were in cuffs, though the fraud had been vast,
And none paid the cost for the ruin they cast.

Banks took their bonuses; charts all glowed with cheer,
As thousands lacked work by the end of the year.
Weasels praised the "rescue" from marble and stone,
But raised new tolls before the aid could be shown.

Fox turned from the boxes stacked high under gold,
His breath curling tight in the dim winter cold.
"They fail," Kit murmured, "yet still land on their feet,
while those without power are swept to the street."

A banner above read, *Be proud and rejoice,*
As if collapse had been the animal's choice.
Beneath it, Starling clutched one jar to her chest,
And the wind blew dust through the square's emptied nest.

Too big to fail; too small to bail.

CHAPTER 22

THE SHRINKING LEAF

Starling rummaged her purse. No crumbs to be had,
She slipped from the square without funds and was sad.
Fox and Kit observed helplessly, feeling worn,
Then walked where the prices made them feel forlorn.

"One Gold-Leaf," said Sparrow, "bought a loaf last week,
But now it takes two, or your pantry grows bleak."
Cricket whispered, "Once this could feed us till May;
Now it won't buy crust or a mouthful today."
The carrots were thinner, the loaves barely rose,
Yet each shop posted the increased fee it chose.
"It's strange," Fox said, "how this money looks the same;
Yet value vanished like frost in summer's flame."

He asked weary Blue Jay, her feathers askew,
"Why does everything cost more now in your view?"
"There is more in circulation," she replied.
"This is why Gold-Leaves' worth has suddenly died."

The Shrinking Leaf

"They claimed," murmured Bear, "that the harvest ran thin,
That drought is to blame for the trouble we're in.
But I've seen the silos, all packed to the brim,
The grain's stacked so high it spills over the rim."

"But didn't the orchards bloom this year?" asked Kit.
"Why make that claim? What do they fear to admit?"
So Fox softly responded next to a yew,
"When funds are printed from thin air, it's not true.
Each leaf that they forge steals a seed from the bowl,
While magpies flash jewels and badgers bankroll."

The beasts still traded goods, confused but resigned,
As costs kept increasing and wealth had declined.
Storm Crow named high demand, weather, and late spawn,
While badgers made currency from dusk until dawn.

At the loan stall, Bronze Badger looked at the scale;
Her body shook with fear as her voice turned frail.
"I don't set these rates, but, if I don't comply,
I'll lose all I've built. I'll be swept out to dry."
A crack in her mask, but it closed in a blink.
She doubled the bite; her paw wrote in with ink.

Stall-banners showed markups no beast could ignore,
While Pearl Magpie swept in with gemstones galore.
She scoffed at the queues and the peasants below,
Then bought her lavish feast in a gaudy show.
"Don't fault the mint," she said with a polished sneer.
"It's envy that drives your complaints every year.
If you had my fortune, you'd sparkle the same.
The rate is the rate, so quit shifting the blame."

Fox held up a Leaf from an elder year's press;
Its gold kept a gleam, though its worth was far less.
"Food grows in nature," Fox said with a long sigh.
"But wealth needs a story to prop up the lie."
He flipped the warm coin in the chill evening sky,
"It's lost so much weight, it might just want to fly.
Worth almost nothing, as if straining to rise:
A bright, empty promise that hoodwinks the eyes."
Kit smirked at the joke, kept it close in hand,
Holding the humor like truth she'd withstand.

She said, "Money-printing has made prices rise.
Too many Gold-Leaves for goods; theft in disguise.
At Mint-Tree we watched how currency was pressed;
Each new batch depressed what our accounts expressed.

The Shrinking Leaf

Bailouts shift losses; the public takes the cost.

They keep the profits; our savings are lost.

Let's head home; we've learned how this deception plays.

Minting with rescues, our future always pays."

More dough, less bread.

CHAPTER 23

NOT CLEARLY ESTABLISHED

A thud split the hush where the mushrooms lay thick:
A gasp, then a rustle, then silence too quick.
Fox froze in the brambles with Kit by his side,
Watching an event no shadow could hide.

Possum lay still near the foot of Grand-Keep's wall,
His basket of moss had weighed nothing at all.
He'd spoken too loud at the wrong time of day,
The wolves claimed he twitched in a threatening way.

They barked, then advanced; no one saw him resist.
"He reached for a rock," was the tale they'd insist.
But Kit saw his paws, folded gentle and low,
One holding a chrysanthemum, white as the snow.

Ringtail stood nearby, his tail twitching in dread,
Eyes wide, like one reading the lines of the dead.
"They plan this," he hissed. "It's a chain they've designed:
Every fence, each gate, preordained and aligned."

Fox gave him a look that was heavy with care.
Ringtail softly muttered, "Don't breathe their air."
Plea Vulture arrived with a scroll in her claw,
And said, "While it's tragic, they followed the law."

She drew closer with a wax seal dipped in red,
"No ruling exists; the complaint is now dead.
No trial has judged such a pattern before,
So the case fails: there is no crime to explore."

A hush moved like fog through the hollows, slate-gray,
As creatures withdrew from the path where he lay.
Fox's teeth locked tight. He could feel the scream burn,
But he swallowed it: there was nowhere to turn.

Kit touched Possum's paw; a fierce tremor took hold.
She drew up her fist while her fury unrolled.
Her anger curled upward, pale ghosts on the breeze,
While the wolves stood unmoved, stone-still like carved trees.

Plea Vulture proclaimed, "No foul play is inferred;
Intent can't be proven beyond what's occurred.
Though painful, the wolves felt a moment of fear,
And fright is a protection when risk is near."

Storm Crow wrote the facts from High-Fence overhead,
And she chirped, "Comply, and you won't end up dead."

But Possum had adhered to every order,
He obeyed, yet died on the castle's border.
Fox glanced towards Grand-Keep where the grief had spread,
Then turned to Kit's wet eyes and quietly pled:
"Wolves serve the law, but they don't have to follow.
They are government's teeth, and they are made to swallow."

Kit's focus stayed fixed on the line of his jaw.
Her thoughts were a verdict, unwritten by law.
Her fingers still shook as she let his paw go,
While the white flower in his grasp sealed her woe.

Immunity breeds impunity.

CHAPTER 24

IN-REM FORFEITURE

One week since Possum had fallen, grief stayed sore.
Kit's silence carried storms Fox could not ignore.
They left the clay den for sunlight's gentle reach
To ease their minds along Rush-Reservoir's beach.

Cardinal flew in with a pouch on his chest:
Eight Gold-Leaves for his brood, a ninth for their nest.
He landed to rest where the reservoir bends.
He offered a song for the forest and friends.

The water shimmered bright, held back by the dam.
Fox watched many fish leap, while Kit played with Clam.
Cardinal's carol danced in loops overhead:
A rare sort of peace in a world ruled by dread.

For one golden moment the air felt like balm;
The river threw diamonds, a day built for calm.
Then through the branches came an unwelcome haze:
Alpha Wolf stepped out with a decisive gaze.

"What's this?" snapped the wolf, and he slashed at the strap;
The pouch spilled its Leaves in a gold-glinting snap.
"This sum is too large for a bird such as you.
We've flagged your description; it matches a few."
"No statute has been broken," Cardinal pled.
"That's what they all say," Alpha Wolf coolly said.

Plea Vulture arrived with the law books in tow.
"This case isn't unique, there's no need for show.
He hasn't been charged, but intent could be there;
The burden is his if he thinks it's unfair."
Next she publicized there along the beachside:
"This form must be signed or your rights are denied.
If you wish to fight, you may pay and request,
But the hearings are slow. We wish you the best."

Kit's voice cracked through the breeze with utter dismay,
"So proof is just something they have waived away?"
Cardinal trembled as his words left his beak.
"I need those Gold-Leaves for my fledglings this week!"
"Then prove they were earned," the wolf said with a grin.
"And evidence that you are not a kingpin."

Fox studied Plea Vulture; her eyelids were tired.
Her duty met pity, thus cooled and rewired.

In-Rem Forfeiture

He caught that brief falter, a heartbeat of stall:
"If Vultures can waver, the system could fall."

Bronze Badger wrote the sum in a log of gray;
She filed the money under *Budget: Mid-May*.
Kit sat in the sand, her focus held in thought.
Cardinal did not object; he never fought.
Kit's resentment bellowed and simmered like coal,
Too worn for a roar, but too deep to console.

The reservoir darkened behind the dam's rim;
One coin lay in silt where the shallows grew dim.
Kit spat, "Wolves claim fairness while bleeding the weak,
And increase their budgets without a critique."

That night in the nest, little cardinals cried;
Their father came hollow, with hunger inside.
He folded them close with a wing turned to brace,
His pouch-string now empty, wind fraying the lace.

Seized on suspicion; sold on commission.

CHAPTER 25

THE HOME YOU NEVER OWN

Fox woke up depressed; the feelings couldn't stray.
He dreamt of wolves prowling on a frigid day.
The Mind-Stump drilled doubts into a decree,
As rats weighed out hours, then chained him to the Mint-Tree.
"I need a long walk," he said, "where waters run."
Kit smiled, "Then I'm coming; we'll share the same sun."

By Twin-Creek's wide fork where the willows divide,
Fox crouched with Kit, morning light at the streamside.
A driftwood slat shelter sat snug to the flow,
Where Otter kept pups from the teeth of the snow.

She worked on the docks loading crates onto boats,
Her pay barely covered her pups' morning oats.
The rates had all doubled, the cost soared sky-high;
The deed was hers but the tax due date slipped by.

Code beavers arrived first with clipboards held high
To measure each beam with a bureaucrat's eye.

The Home You Never Own

"This shelter's too close to the streambed below;
The rules say it's risky for runoff or flow."
Then Mint Badger arrived to foreclose her home,
And told her she had to abandon this loam.

Plea Vulture descended with law books of brass,
Her glasses reflected the dew on the grass.
"This is not done out of malice," she maintained,
"but rules must apply or their meaning is strained."
She tacked up a notice: "This dwelling's unsound,
And taxes were not paid for use of this ground."

Otter went silent as her pups pressed in near;
She gathered their blankets and swallowed her fear.
Fox said, "We'll go with you till you find a place."
Kit nodded, "We'll help you find another space."

They searched through the forest for somewhere to stay,
But signs and restrictions drove Otter away.

No tents are permitted, a sign near the ridge.
No camping underneath the government bridge.
Permits are needed to slumber under trees,
And fines will apply if you lounge without these.

They wandered past posts where the briars grew deep,
Past hammocks of canvas and dens made to sleep.
They had entered the Shade-Slum, their only choice,
And then prayed to God in a desperate voice.

A fire dimly burned near a well-weathered knoll,
And there sat Tortoise with black beans in his bowl.
"I've lived here for eleven seasons," he said,
"No fees to pay when you rest with no bed."

"Eat with me," he called, "and please rest where it's warm."
Otter stood stiff, pride enveloping her form.
"I work hard for my young," she said, jaw set tight.
She turned down the offer and left the firelight.

Later, the wind gnawed; her pups could not sleep;
She returned to the circle with tears she kept deep.

The tamarins shared what the dam could not own:
A blanket, a bowl, and a low, steady tone.
"Thank you," Otter whispered, the words like a sting.
She learned that aid is a hand, not a gold ring.

Fox sat by the fire as the frost bit the ground,
While her pups clung together, faint heat around.

The Home You Never Own

No den had been granted, no mercy, no light,
Just trembling cold bodies exposed to the night.

"Who builds for the poor when the costs climb so high?"
Kit growled from the circle with flame in her eye.
"Who deems one as worthy and others as strays?
Who claims there is no room while the rich pave ways?"

She cupped her paws to the ember's orange seam.
The heat licked her pads like a midsummer dream.
Fox watched the light cradle her fingers like rain,
And stored it for winter when doubt would remain.

At dawn they walked back where the creeks split the shore;
The hut now stood empty, swept clean to the core.
One plank bore a scuff where the pots used to fall,
And a fresh-stamped *FOR SALE* sign nailed to the wall.

'Owned' is 'owed' with an 'N.'

CHAPTER 26

RELIEF IN DISGUISE

At first light, they walked to the market for bread
For dear Otter's pups, to see them truly fed.
Fox pressed on the old purse from the Mint-Tree's vault,
And swore to mend hunger, not forgive one fault.
A flag rose high over the heart of Leaf-Square,
"Relief for the hoopoes!" Storm Crow cried with flair.
With white and blue streamers and drums beating hard,
The planners then drew crowds and brought in the guard.

Fox eased through the concourse with Kit at his side,
Her ears on the speeches, her eyes opened wide.
They passed donation bins, hearing cheers in air,
"Let's listen," said Kit. "I don't trust this affair."

"The hoopoes are helpless," Sly Weasel declared,
"Beset by evil terrorists, starved and scared.
They need our support, our defense, and our grain,
To feed them brings peace; to object is disdain."

Relief in Disguise

Bluff Owl spoke softly on a column of slate,
"Their forest is fragile, their timing is late.
We can rebuild their schools and pay those who've died;
To fix what was lost, we will stand at their side."
Her voice made a crack that a script could not hide;
One feather-tip twitched as her gaze slid aside.

Writ Vulture swore with a voice not to mislead,
"Humanitarian aims are creeds that we heed.
With food comes a footnote; with funding, a string.
Their loyalty ensures what our flag will bring."
Grease Boar rolled in with contracts bound in sealed wax.
"New aid allocations," he puffed through the cracks.
He winked at Shade Spider; the deal is all done.
The ink had long dried before talks had begun.

Head Hoopoe stepped beside Sly Weasel on stage,
His feathers all flared with tribute and assuage.
He bowed as required, though his gaze did not drop;
He'd done this before, and the gifts did not stop.
"We need just one base," said Shade Spider nearby,
"To cinch your protection from threats from the sky.
One pipeline for trade, a clearing for war drones,
And rights to a slice of your ancestral zones."

The crowd clapped on as Sly Weasel blessed the day;
Yet what relief would not give, it took away.
For this was a bargain, a chain in disguise,
And peace was enforced with conditions and lies.

Fox watched as the hoopoes received their new bombs
To rain on their foes without question or qualms.
Relief carts rolled onward, their emblems aglow,
The kindness on top and the weapons below.

Fox said, "This '*aid*' underwrites rockets and guns;
Our wages are siphoned to corporate funds."

"What about our own roofs?" Starling retorted.
Kit replied, "That relief has been exported."

"The war will never end," Fox muttered to Kit,
"There is always one group who is deemed unfit.
They rename the battle, they reshape the plea;
But they constantly need a new enemy."

Kit's voice was quiet: "Is aid just for control?"
Fox's eyes burned bright as the thought left his soul:

Relief in Disguise

"When peace comes and there's no foe for their parade,
Will they mold a villain just to hew their blade?"

Foreign aid; domestic charade.

CHAPTER 27

CRATER DAY

A moon cycle passed since aid had left Leaf-Square,
Fox paced with Kit, breathing the September air.
Rush-Reservoir silvered behind the stone gate;
Wild-Grove lay ahead, would harvest have to wait?

At eight-forty-six, thunder tore the green wide.
At nine-oh-three, shock rolled the valley's broad side.
The forest held stillness; even sunlight stayed,
Black smoke blooming where tall cedars had once swayed.
Fox felt the cold tighten; Kit breathed, "This is fear."
Then Owl-Spire's horn rang, "All creatures, gather here."

Great Owl called it terror, "An enemy's hand!
The skunks have attacked us, they've struck Twin-Vales' land!"
His phrases came ready, too polished to mourn,
Like headlines prepared long before they were born.

Mockingbird described what she saw in the blast,
"Two figures in cloaks running strangely too fast."

Crater Day

Shade Spider said, "That's an artifact, not proof.
Lens flare can turn two shadows to a mere spoof."

Ringtail, eyes wide, tugged hard at Fox's furred sleeve:
"I saw two black spiders! You've got to believe!"

The beasts hooted and laughed, "He's simply absurd."
But Kit, not the crowd, knew the hard truth she heard.
Balm Snake observed, "Acute stress. This reads untrue:
Your mind scripts motives that doubt drives you to do."

Masked Weasel announced, "Leaf-Square this night we meet
To speak for the fallen and keep faith complete."
Yet Fox caught his glances twice toward the far east,
And his jaw clenched hard, for a heartbeat at least.

Sly Weasel led a vigil with flags in rain;
She offered heartfelt "thoughts and prayers" to the slain.
"Our homeland was bombed twice," she said with glass eyes.
"Now unity matters, no questions, no whys."
She vowed, "At first bell we will act to enclose;
Tomorrow we'll seal what the enemy chose."

Storm Crow read the roll-call of the newly dead,
"Nineteen terrorists died from the bombs," she said.

"No one knew their motives or whence they had come;
Yet verdicts declared, they're the ones it came from.
We've found a skunk ID in the fire's remains,
Although the heat had melted iron and chains."

When cinders burned low and the crying was done,
Fox tugged Kit to climb where the two vales are one.
From Spine-Ridge heights they saw both valleys below;
Two craters steamed, yet a third one was aglow.

Kit whispered, "Two blasts we heard, yet here are three.
The third had no rumble, only scorched debris.
If two cut ground," she asked, "then what carved this pit?
What split the earth downward without any hit?"

Fox replied, "I don't know. Let's sleep for the night.
At dawn, we'll go to congress to hear our plight."

At first light they took seats in the Leaf-Dome's ring;
Sly Weasel read laws with a sorrow-clad sting.
"A bill has been drafted for national peace:
Compliance is kindness; let terror now cease."

The statute passed swiftly, its phrasing severe:
To question the record is harmful to hear.

Crater Day

For freedom to flourish, all must be observed,
Security first, and dissent shall be swerved.
Then beavers strung sensor wires through boughs and glen,
While weasels proclaimed, *It won't happen again.*

On Leaf-Dome steps, all of Congress stood aligned,
Ruby and Cobalt weasels, twin chiefs, entwined.
They sang the forest anthem, raising the song;
The Thirteen on the balcony sang along.

As the final chord faded beyond the hall,
Crane asked, "Where were wolves when we sounded the call?"
Alpha Wolf snapped, "*Peace Act* demands compliance."
The bailiffs closed in, citing her defiance.

They bound Crane in silence and marched her past stone;
Her question fell hard like a bird without bone.
Fox and Kit trailed Crane to the arch of Knot-Hall,
Where truth was untied and the gavel let fall.

Plea Vulture in robes convened court without pause,
For Crane, who "sowed distrust" in the sanctioned cause.
"You are free to speak," the judge said with a frown,
"But choose the correct time, and keep your voice down."

Crane was found guilty by the jury of peers.
As wolves cuffed her wings, she was scolded with jeers.
They dragged her to Thorn-Hold, the rat-owned stronghold,
Where cells swell their ledgers and mercy is sold.

Fox turned toward Kit, who was no longer there.
Then Slate Wolf stepped beside him and snarled, "Beware.
I caught your scent inside the courtroom's stale stone,
Mint-Tree, Grand-Keep, Wild-Grove," she warned him alone.

She had trampled away and Kit reappeared,
Fox barely eased, but it was worse than he'd feared.
"Are you alright?" she murmured, pale and afraid.
"I think I'm marked," he said. "Keep close to the shade."

She muttered, "I can't tell what's real anymore."
He sighed, "That is the goal of an endless war.
They call it protection, then watch every door.
If surveillance makes us safe, what's freedom for?"

Rights to rites, by writes.

CHAPTER 28

THE BITTERSWEET CLINIC

The forest had fallen to muffled refrain,
Since Crater Day's blast left its lingering stain.
Kit rested uneasy in the morning's gloom,
While Fox perceived an uncomfortable doom.

Ringtail kept muttering, "The skunks weren't to blame;
The spiders were there, I remember the frame.
They marked where the blast would collapse Twin-Vales' side,
And vanished away before the stones had died."
Then two wolves arrived to escort him away,
and disappeared into Moss-Care's green archway.
Kit's hackles rose sharp, "He's no danger, no threat!"
But Fox pulled her back, "They will make you regret."

In the hospital, Shade Spider's voice turned severe,
"Residual trauma has festered his fear.
Some thoughts, when relived, will unravel the whole,
Let's quiet these echoes that darken his soul."

Balm Snake, in a coat trimmed with brass at the seams,
Unveiled purple vials that shimmered like dreams.
"This new sugar is much gentler than the last.
It mutes dire ideas gathering too fast.
It quells heavy notions before they take hold,
And leaves no hard edges, no bold thought controlled."

Shade Spider hung charts from a branch made of wire,
With photos and notes from before the big fire.
"We found revisiting prolongs their distress,
So we subtly guide them to forgetfulness."
Ringtail was ordered to guzzle from the glass.
"The pain," Balm Snake assured him, "will sway and pass.
Your thoughts are jagged. The burden's far too high.
Let solace enfold you, and let bitterness lie."

He drank, then grew serene, his eyes glazed in sleep;
His arms lost their twitch, and his murmur sank deep.
Upon discharge, he recalled no bombs or flame,
Nor Spiders, he swore, had been part of the game.

Kit advanced to the doorway, "Ringtail, it's Kit."
He blinked at her face like the name didn't fit.
"Do I know you from somewhere?" He searched, frowned slow,
"Remind me... your name? I'm sorry, I don't know."

"It's Kit," she repeated; the word wouldn't land.
"It's Kit," once again, with a shake in her hand.

He offered a smile, confused, helpless, and small;
The sugar-slick haze had unthreaded it all.

Fox watched from the shadows, his thoughts tightly bound,
Kit's eyes on the mist curling close to the ground.
"Do thoughts make the forest unstable to grow?"
"They fear what can't be controlled," he replied low.
"They'll claim it's for healing, a cure for the scar,
But comfort that blinds is a war's unseen spar."

Balm Snake marked her case on a clipboard with pride,
"Subject now stable. The disruption has died."
Shade Spider leaned close from a branch in the tree,
And signed to administer dose number three.

Great Owl gave a gripping speech outside to quell:
"The clinic has helped those who used to rebel.
Their pain has been reduced. Their hearts beat in tune;
They've dropped the theories that once dimmed the moon."

Fox sighed as Storm Crow wrote a neat, cheerful phrase:
"Thanks to New-Sugar, calm has brightened our days."

Yet creatures all nodded, no doubt in their eye;
For memory fades when it's taught not to try.

"If words make them hurt, is the medicine harm?"
Kit asked as the fog wrapped the ward in its arm.
Fox whispered, "If peace needs a pill to exist,
Then what kind of war did the clinic assist?"

The cure was recited as mercy, not blame;
Yet soon after, voices were silenced the same.
The skunks felt the weight of the rumors take hold,
Their futures have been half-written in the cold.

Calm the nerves; calm the nerve.

CHAPTER 29

CONDITIONAL FREEDOM

A week on, they walked the Free-Way with the crowd,
If you see something, say something signs flashed loud.
A new bill was tabled; debate would start soon,
Fox and Kit waited as the clock struck noon.

Beneath the Leaf-Dome's glass, etched in gilt veneer,
Fox crouched beside Kit, straining both eye and ear.
Through green-tinged panes, the weasel congress convened,
Debating which freedoms would subtly be weaned.

Sly Weasel stood atop a marble-lined ramp:
"To guard against threats, some must go to a camp.
Relocation is safety, not blame or fear.
It is a privilege to keep living here."

Fat Rat, who owned Thorn-Hold, amended the clause;
Grease Boar at his shoulder then cued the applause.
The clerk read "approved" as the roll-call was cast,
And skunks in the gallery braced for the blast.

A mother hugged her pups with a little squeal.
A wolf checked the scent, then put them behind steel.

"They haven't been charged," cried Bunting from the pine.
"It's for our protection," came Alpha Wolf's line.
"When motives are shadowed, we act to ensure;
Suspicion alone is enough to secure."

Fox tugged Kit, "Let's follow and see what's foretold."
They trailed wolves to Safe-Patch upwind near Thorn-Hold.

The camps were enclosed with no locks on the gates,
But wolves stood outside with identical plates.
No sentence was judged, and no trial was held,
Mere patterns and details that the courts compelled.

Plea Vulture looked down with a voice soft and clear,
"It's not guilt, but risk, that has brought skunks in here.
Their rights are intact with conditions applied;
They may still appeal, though the last was denied."

A young skunk looked up, "What offense did we cause?"
She shrugged and replied, "We're enforcing new laws.
With or without guilt, it's a fairness decree.
We all must make sacrifices to stay free."

Mint Badger explained beneath an office shield,
"Their tokens are frozen until they are healed.
It's only precaution, for safety of all,
Until we determine their danger is small."

Fox hid with Kit as the sun had lost its heat,
While tents began to fill with slow, shuffling feet.

The breeze brushed their whiskers, the sky turning gray,
And Fox said, "They can take liberty away.
If freedom is granted to count or endure,
Then they're not rights, just control made to look pure."

Yet from the far fence came a soft hopeful hum,
A song from the camps like a low-beating drum.
By lantern-lit tarps they had opened a school
To barter new skills under nobody's rule.

Kit watched the small market rise up out of dust,
And warmth broke her guard like a hinge losing rust.
A skunk pulled a splinter from a wolf pup's paw,
Then tied it up snug with a forgiving claw.

Kit's heart caught the sight, not of fear, but of flame:
A promise that none there would vanish in shame.

THE FOX WHO WONDERED WHY

Fox felt a tight band cinch shut around his lungs,
The tents like closed throats, the watchtowers' sharp tongues.
His sight tunneled narrow, the ground seemed to tilt;
The future choked closed like Rush-Dam clogged with silt.

Kit set her warm paw on his ribs, "Count the breeze.
Four leaves in, four leaves out; match willow-wind's ease.
Name earth, name the moonlight, name clover and stone,
Name weather, name water: you are not alone."

He breathed to her cadence, the tightness unclenched,
The depression inside had no longer wrenched.
The lanterns went dim, but their pulses kept time;
Two steady small beats in a camp without crime.

Liberty by waiver will waver.

CHAPTER 30

THE REWRITING MIRROR

They left with the skunks' song still warm in their ears,
A hum that cut quiet through gathering fears.
But on Sly-Path's bend, where the roots gripped the ground,
A strange new device arrived without a sound.

A mirror stood resting on eight woven spars,
Its frame strung with web-lines that glistened like stars.
Dark tethers were woven in lattices high,
As spiders mapped thoughts in the hush of the sky.
Scents, gaits, and heartbeats were sifted into codes;
Tags bloomed beside faces in fanning white nodes.

Each strand traced a spark through its branching array,
Then fixed it into glass while facts fell away.
The network fed upward to Pattern-Web's crown;
A thousand bright threads gathered every thought down.

The crowd pressed in close with a reverent cheer,
Each gazing to glimpse their approved image here.

A pollen-small fleck kissed each muzzle in line;
It tracked each footfall's path, it drank every sign.

"It shows you at your best," trilled Stork full of pride,
"And smooths all the rest so you're safe deep inside."
"It quiets my dreams," murmured Reindeer in place,
"I follow its glow and keep pace with its grace."

"She's smiling," Kit whispered, "but something's obscured:
Her eyes look too empty; her joy feels assured."

Fox stepped toward the black glass, breath held and lean,
And it handed him back a version scrubbed clean.
His whiskers were trimmed and his teeth were brushed white;
His doubts were pressed flat and edges folded tight.
His color was not correct, his smile too wide;
His tail was too stiff, and his spirit too tied.

The fox, they'd written, was compliant and thin;
It nodded on cue like a puppet within.
A fear bit him: "*If I accept what they write,
I'll turn into the thing I have vowed to fight.*"
Kit saw false face the mirror chose to display,
And then marked the deceit; she filed it away.

The Rewriting Mirror

"Why does it alter me?" he asked with a frown.
"It's better this way," said Bluff Owl, flying down.
"The truth can be vile, confusing and unkind.
This mirror learns to quell the storm in your mind.
Besides," she continued, her spectacles square,
"The spiders approve every angle with care.
What's shown has been vetted for clarity's sake.
Too much raw reflection could cause one to break."

A pause crossed her beak; her cadence slipped awry;
Kit saw the doubt and held that fracture close by.

"Perhaps," Fox responded, "what you call the truth
Is more like a window that rewrites our youth."

But Fox wasn't sure, so he circled around,
And turned the pane slowly to face rocky ground.
It flickered, then sputtered, then darkened to black.
No image, no signal, no echo came back.

"You broke it!" cried Shade Spider. "Our lovely beam!
That tool is our record, our standard, our dream.
It syncs to the Pattern-Web, kept in the cloud:
Your changes are logged; noncompliance is loud."

"If protocol logs me," Fox said with a glare,
"Then freedom's a fraud that never played fair."

Shade Spider leaned close with a needle-bright smile,
"Your actions are flagged; we've watched you for a while.
One tug on this thread and the pack knows your trail;
Your scent will map routes while the networks surveil."

Kit felt the tag prickle like nettles that burn.
"To the woods," Fox rasped, "run now and don't turn."
They tore through the thickets, the meshwork went dim,
And wolves raised a howl from the far-rising rim.

They parted the reach of the Pattern-Web's span,
In brambles too twisted for watchers to scan.
He asked himself, "*If they edit what we need,*
Are choices our own, or what they choose to seed?"

Edits become edicts.

CHAPTER 31
RECORDED CONTROL

Fox crept after Kit down a root-tangled bend,
Where the trees pressed close and the path seemed to end.
Fog gripped the canopy; the ferns sank to shade.
The path pinched narrow; the moss began to fade.
They blundered along into marsh-shadowed ground;
Beneath green-lit lanterns, creatures made no sound.

"Do you know where we are?" Kit breathed at his side.
Fox murmured, "Mute-Moor, I think." His stare went wide.
He stepped closer, his senses coming alight,
And spotted an oddness that snagged at his sight.
An oak held a lens, fine as dew on a thread,
That captured each breath and each turn of the head.

Kit touched the small object hidden in the tree.
"It's only a tool that imprisons the free.
It trims what you think so no doubts can survive,
And buries freedom that fights to stay alive."

Her claws slid deep into the bark's softened seam,
And snapped the thin wire like breaking a bad dream.
The lens gave a spark, then a hiss, and went black,
The Pattern-Web's watching eye cut from its track.

Bullfrog's throaty croak swelled to something near cheer;
Goldfinch stood taller, her aspect losing fear.
Salamander said low, "They'll know you've undone."
Kit said, "Let them know. Its purpose helps no one."

Bullfrog croaked quietly, his voice barely there,
"They capture your speaking, then render you bare.
At one time I taught the school choir how to sing,
But the songs that I picked were deemed as a sting.
The spiders," he whispered, "hold threads from the past.
They braid each small slip into cables that last."

Bullfrog, off-guard, hummed a soulful, crooked strain,
The *Peace-River* ballad, now rattled with pain.
Fox flinched at the off-key notes crooned in the song,
And ached for the version that carried him strong.

Goldfinch glanced down at the bronze ring on her foot.
"They filmed me once, when I gave honest input.

Recorded Control

I work at the Knot-Hall, my tone must be tight;
My words must be filtered to prove I'm polite.
The recordings," she cried, "will circle for years.
They keep me compliant; they broker my fears.
It's just an agreement, be still and obey.
They tell me that silence keeps danger away."

Then spoke Salamander, her stare hard and wet,
"They film every creature who stirs a regret.
The beavers install them in rafter and beam,
Where each misplaced murmur flows into the stream."

"But why do they spy?" Fox asked, clenching his jaw.
"To make you correct, without breaking the law,
And alter your speech so your signals align,
Without errors in the Pattern-Web's design."

They said goodbyes and left where moonlight ran free,
Past shadows that whispered of what might now be.
And Kit, with a glint that was fierce, not just sly,
Said, "If the wardens can fall, so can their lie."

They drifted through dusk and returned to their door,
Fox banked the coals; Kit set packs on the clay floor.

An owl-post arrived for Kit, penned with gold quill,
"*Grind-Bluff, Merit Trial, come assess your skill.*"
"I'm going to see what's judged," Kit said, fierce-bright;
Fox, wary and afraid, stepped back from the light.

Surveil to curtail.

CHAPTER 32

THE BLUFFED RUNGS

Kit led Fox to a cliff-face too steep to climb,
Where creatures scaled ladders to escape the grime.
Great Owl sat atop Grind-Bluff with eyes of gold,
Declaring, "This forest rewards the most bold!"

Rove Goat raised a scroll and proclaimed from a log,
"Success is for beasts who can push through the slog.
The climb builds your virtue," he bellowed with pride,
"The slow and the weak should stay off the cliffside."
He glanced to the ledge, with his hoof near his head.
His lecture slowed when doubt grew from the script he'd said.

The Thirteen were perched where no ladder was placed,
Each beast with a title, well-groomed and well-graced.
They clinked their fine glasses while wolves blocked the trail,
For none who climbed up were allowed to prevail.

The stairs were obeyed by animals below,
Who thought they'd be safe if they just ran the show.

Each ladder rung taught them which thoughts to dismiss,
And consent grew thick in a system like this.

Bobcat in stride slipped and fell into the mud.
"Pick up the pace!" snapped Peacock. "It's only blood!"
"Hardship builds character," he squawked with a grin,
Then turned from the slope where nobody could win.

Snail paused for a breath. Falcon shouted, "Don't stop!
Rewards are for those who make it to the top!"
Kestrel kept tally; Meadowlark marked the late.
Each one had their reason to regulate fate.

"Thrush shoved poor Toad off," said a Bighorn with dread,
"For claiming he hungered for just a dry bed.
Then up went the Thrush with a grin on his face,
While Toad lay below, erased without a trace."

Fox watched Lemming clamber toward the first rung,
but stones slipped away where his chances had hung.
"No masters are in sight," he said with dismay,
"But fear keeps them climbing the same broken way."

Kit reached for a rung, but was caught in a snare.
Falcon's rope coiled tightly with a raptor's glare.

The Bluffed Rungs

"Your form is improper," he barked from his seat,
While others piled judgment in sweltering heat.

Fox bent to release her, his tone sharp and low,
"This ascent is staged, dressed as virtue's true show.
They praise your ambition, then rig every test,
Till you blame yourself for the rope 'round your chest."

Kit's gaze climbed the summit, her jaw set like stone,
"I'll test what they boast; I will do this alone."

She reached up again, her focus on the climb,
But Fox caught her wrist. "Please, not here. Not this time.
If every rung's priced in another beast's pain,
Then what do you gain when you reach their domain?"

She yanked; the rope tightened and scored through her fur
A thin, angry band where the fibers would burr.
She hissed, licked her wrist till the stinging would fade,
Then swallowed her anger, tempered it to a blade.

Fox sank into gray; sound thinned to distant rain.
The crowd blurred to smudge; each thought dragged like a chain.
His grip loosened; his ribs felt something shatter:
If I lose her, nothing I've done will matter.

He stared at the top as the banners unfurled;
She bleeds for a height that won't welcome her world.

She edged ten rungs up; the slope shivered below.
Fox folded inside; time oozed heavy and slow.
The knot slipped then snapped; she plunged and struck the ground.
A crack lit her flank; breath fled without a sound.

Fox jolted from dread; the fog splintered like glass.
He lifted her slowly, picked a path through grass.
"To Moss-Care," he vowed, "hold fast; breathe river air."
"We're going now," he said. "I will get you there."

Rung by rung; wrung by rung.

CHAPTER 33

COSTLY CURE

Fox carried Kit, her breathing feeble and slow,
Her flank faintly tremored with a bruising glow.
Inside Moss-Care chilled of alcohol and ice,
Balm Snake wore a white coat and named her own price.
She bowed with a smile, "You've come to the right place.
The damage can be cured. Please give me some space.
I will mix comfrey with mint till it combines;
It eases the pain and aligns the bloodlines."

Fox offered the payment he'd scraped from his store.
Snake's eyes stared blankly at the tiles on the floor.
"This treatment is for the creatures who can sign;
No comfort is given till you sign that line."

Plea Vulture descended with forms in her claw,
Each page had fine print that resembled the law.
She stamped it and voiced, "No insurance was shown.
Without the right form, she is fully alone."

Fox barked, "But she's young! How was she meant to know?
There must be exceptions, you profit from woe!"

Snake purred, "I'm the doctor, not keeper of fates.
I offer medicine. The contract dictates."

Plea Vulture slid papers, "Mark here for the debt.
Therapy begins when agreement is met.
You're welcome to file a petition and wait;
We process filings at a prescriptive rate."
Her quill traced circles; she brushed one tear away.
She closed the case file; her wings refused to sway.

Oriole limped in from the back room with gauze,
A cast on his wing and a twitch in his claws.
He whispered to Fox, "They could help her for free,
But charity ranks far beneath the decree.
Doctors once promised to give healing to all:
The wealthy, the broken, the wing-clipped, the small.
But now life is sold like a tincture of sin;
Their oath is a skin they've long shed from within."

Fox's eyes inflamed as Kit's chest barely stirred.
Balm Snake put away the dose without a word.

Costly Cure

"Bring Gold-Leaves or endorse the fee on the page,
And maybe her lesion will loosen its cage."

They walked out the front door; her breath was still light.
The sky outside dimmed to a darkening night.
He set her on straw by a broken glass jar,
His face warped in waves like a forgotten star.

A dire, fleeting thought skimmed the wavering brim;
Her life would go on, though it may exclude him.
It flashed and it faded, no lure and no art;
He gripped to her cadence to anchor his heart.
One notch steadier, there he counted and kept
An ebb he could hold while his ache barely slept.

Kit observed Fox as the pain left her frame,
"This was mild, but the next injury might maim.
You pay with your coin or your freedom in kind,
That's how they ensure you stay caught in their bind."

She clutched at his paw with a feverish plea,
"We've seen it in ladders, in mirrors, in me.
If we don't keep walking, the leash only grows,
And they'll count each heartbeat the ledger still knows."

A ragged rip lingered along her left side,
A pale crescent scar where the ripping had dried.
She hid a deep fear she refused to impart:
That one day their parting would fracture her heart.

The wind tasted sharp with a hospital chill,
Yet under the dread was a flicker of will.
Fox felt it inside, like a coal yet to flame:
"This fight isn't ours, yet we're stuck in this game."

Debt for a dose; dose for a debt.

CHAPTER 34

FOG OF FORMS

Two weeks had slowly eased the wound on Kit's side,
And her color crept back like a turning tide.
Fox said, "You're steadier. Let's fetch daily bread,
But first to Knot-Hall, then check on Otter's shed."

They came for the papers that Moss-Care required,
To apply for insurance that they desired.
Fox and Kit approached where a placard was placed,
All Questions Begin Here, it announced, bold-faced.

They entered Knot-Hall where vultures dressed in gray.
One said, "Fill out each page of Form Nineteen-A."
Fox scribbled his name, but the lines blurred and bent.
"Submit that in blue ink with given consent."
"But who will give me consent?" Fox asked a Moose.
She pointed to Bluebird, who pointed to Goose.

"You'll need a notary from the Desk of Roots,
And one embossed stamp from the Guild of Disputes.

Then submit the pile to the Registrar's Sleigh,
Which opens up exclusively each leap day."

Gilt Magpie swept in with his scroll like a prize,
And slid past the queue under the clerks' dull eyes.
A vulture intoned, "Use the side door, my friend.
We'll seal this and you'll be approved by day's end."
He watched the long lines, beaks chapped by hunger's cold,
And paused, half-ashamed, as pity pricked his gold.

Lark turned to Fox, clutching papers wrapped in twine,
"I've begged for repairs since the flood in O-Nine.
But my claim was returned for a "misspelling,"
Though the water spoke when it claimed my dwelling."

Hope dropped inside Fox like a stone from a height,
It could wreck a life, and he felt tight with fright.

Jackdaw said, "I applied twice for a trade stall,
But they misplaced my bid in the permit hall.
They cleared my license, but not for my seed stand,
Then fined me for setting up on the wrong land."

They wandered down halls coiled like ivy on trees,
With footnotes and levies stacked in legalese.

Fog of Forms

The walls held up codes that no creature could read,
While vultures declared, "You lack follow-through speed."

A tunnel was drawn with a labyrinth's braid,
Surveyed by the beavers where logic decayed.
They mapped every sheet with redundant intent
To funnel requests through a proof of descent.

Desks bristled with levers, signs jingled on cue,
And deeds were buried in bureaucracy's glue.
A beaver in goggles said, "Wait in this line,
Unless you want Section B-seven, not nine."

Kit griped to Fox as her blood began to boil,
"If they can't deny you, they'll drown you in toil.
They wrap up the simple in layers that bind.
Not all rights are cut; it's the strength of your mind."

Fox slammed the last sheet on the counter in place,
Each box and signature, a joke to his face.
"If sanity cracks before help even lands,
Is the point to assist or to tie up our hands?"

Kit's patience turned steel as she gathered the thread:
"Let's leave here now to go purchase our corn bread.

If paperwork chokes us, we'll write in the dark,
Off-book, off their ledgers, with marrow for mark."

Fox met Kit's gaze. Her flank injury had eased,
But her breath still caught in the cool autumn breeze.
His panic wasn't lost, and time still felt drawn.
Yet the path wasn't blocked; a way to go on.

Queue patience; cue penance.

CHAPTER 35

DEEDS IN THE DARK

The red-clay den breathed slow as hazy light bled,
"Please take me to see *The Book of Roles*," Kit said.
Fox rubbed his shard-scar, then nodded. "We will go.
But it's filled with lies: that's all you need to know."

They crossed into Peace-Glade where the leaf-shade pressed,
And sunlight poured warm and their spirits felt blessed.
Fox was leading Kit to the hidden Key-Cave,
When he held her back and froze, not feeling brave.

Ahead, where the path reached the cave, stood Grease Boar.
He looked about, and stepped softly through the door.
Others entered after with heads slightly bowed,
Their footfalls kept faint, though no crowd was allowed.

Kit slipped past the stones and crept to the far edge.
Fox begged, "Please, don't go. Don't step to that next ledge."
She met his eyes: "I'm going in. Step aside."
Fox followed, heart racing, to stay by her side.

The arch was cut deep in a moss-covered wall,
With vines draped like chains in a shadow-soaked hall.
They hid out of sight; not a candle would glow,
Behind worn books on shelves all stacked in a row.

Grease Boar sat at a desk with a leather case.
He opened it up and set a scroll in place.
Masked Weasel stepped up with a bureaucrat's stance:
"This didn't happen, but I'll take the advance."

A Leaf-stack was passed with a paw that looked sure.
Its ink smelled like laws that had learned to obscure.
Masked Weasel signed quickly to shift what was true.
"Your quarry's now safe." A distaste trembled through.

Writ Vulture arrived with a clause to delete;
A footnote removed so it wouldn't repeat.
"This lapse could be fined," he began to protest.
Boar slid him Gold-Leaves. "Then the matter can rest."

Mint Badger looked up with his tightly wound roll.
"Compliance," he muttered, "is always the goal."
"A minor revision," Boar grinned with a shrug.
"Wild-Grove is mine, just sweep it under the rug."

Deeds in the Dark

Arch Beaver stepped in with his blueprints unrolled:
"That orchard is closed, except now it is sold."
His map showed a scuff where the waterways curved:
"A harmless update; the record's preserved."

Great Owl finally spoke, his glasses agleam,
"Stability first! We hold to what we deem."
Grease Boar chuckled low with a shake of his mane,
"Then bless this mining deed; it keeps us humane."

Storm Crow perched above with a script in her beak,
Declaring, "Tomorrow, the Tilt-Mine will peak.
We'll flood them with news of a scandal so wide;
The creatures will gossip while the grove will slide."

Fox didn't see her there. He stiffened with dread.
Shade Spider thumbed a bulky folder in red.
She tapped on three letters spelling K-I-T.
He knew what it meant: *There'd be no amnesty*.

Then Kit stifled as Shade Spider set it near;
The binder marked "Kit." Its letters felt severe.
The name burned in ink, and it vanished from sight,
Shut in a coffer and taken from the light.

Fox leaned toward Kit as elites slipped away,

"They plot in the dark, and perform in the day."

Kit whispered, "That file... what's the reason or law?"

Fox shrugged. "This isn't something that I foresaw."

She squared her small shoulders, her voice low, exact,

"They can write me in logs, but I won't be cracked."

Sign the lie; re-sign the land.

CHAPTER 36

THE TILTED GROVE

Two moons in the den, they spoke little, kept small,
Till the itch for truth outgrew that quiet wall.
They followed the hush of Sly-Path's narrow seam
To verify the Key-Cave's candle-lit scheme.

Fox and Kit headed for where the berries grew
With abundant fruits and violets pale blue.
Now engines unstitched earth, the soil pulled apart
Within the Wild-Grove where there once lived a heart.

The roots had been severed, the beetles were gone.
Loons circled, confused, in the chemical dawn.
And carved through the stand was a wide-open wound,
A mine where the trees were relentlessly pruned.

Metallic dust bit the back of Fox's throat;
Hot oil filmed his tongue in a tar-bitter coat.
It tasted like gearwork ground into hard slag,
A smear you could swallow that clung like a rag.

Kit pointed to drills where the bedrock was split
And muttered, "Grease Boar owns this whole grove, each bit."

Fat Rat with a drill and a claw caked in grime,
Grunted, "Quarry deeper! The resin's in prime!"
Behind him, the saplings lay trampled and torn,
As he barked out quotas to crews bruised and worn.
"Extract more," he squeaked, in his rust-coated vest,
"For harvest and glory, for war's endless quest.
The lube feeds motors, the black drives all the lines,
And powers the teeth of the profit designs."

With backs bent and blistered, the gophers moved stone,
As slugs hunted oil in the cracks all alone.
"Keep up your pace!" rasped Dock Rat, pointing a claw.
"Production is progress. Efficiency's law."
A heartbeat of doubt released her rigid palm;
She tallied their blisters, then chose to be calm.

Great Owl, high above on a scaffold of steel,
Proclaimed to the workers, "The Tilt-Mine will heal!
The forest requires a sacrifice be made;
The woodlands will return once the bills are paid.
We dig to ensure that all creatures survive.
The land must be priced if the system will thrive."

The Tilted Grove

Kit clutched Fox's side as the machines groaned near,
"What did they do to this place? What happened here?"
He watched as the stumps formed a graveyard in rows,
"They say it's the cost, but who reaps what it sows?"
Grouse replied, "The woods will return, have no fear.
The trees only sleep while they're harvesting here."

"Why do this?" Fox questioned Buck next to a stack.
"To keep debt collectors," he sighed, "off my back.
They say it's our duty to siphon the land,
Or anarchy will destroy the laws that stand."
But Fox heard the bedrock sigh low like a ghost,
Breathing out grief for what had mattered the most.
He crouched under a tree with a sap-slicked face,
And saw that the orchard had lost more than space.

Kit leaned on a fir as the twilight turned gold,
And whispered, "I'm sorry," as sorrow took hold.
Her voice cracked with gloom. She cried into the bark,
"They've traded your verdant for a deeper dark.
They take from the forest and poison its grace,
Then bury the loss in ledgers they embrace."

On steel catwalks, Great Owl raised a file dark red.
Fox read Kit's name and fright filled his chest with lead.

Kit pressed to the trunk, her tears staining the grain.
She kept her eyes down; gloom pooled and would not drain.

On panic's steep ledge, his breath stuttered and shrank;
One thought touched his heart and the whole body sank.
Kit leveled her gaze, set him steady to stand,
"Come home," she said gently, "take hold of my hand."

He hid the file's secret like cinders that burn.
It settled in silence, a cold, unseen urn.
She spoke of the mine as they crossed the ravine.
He nodded and stared where the pines had been green.

By night her tears hardened, hurt tempered to heat.
Her jaw set to iron, her stride found a beat.
She faced the foul rigs like a storm drawn to break.
Each step threw a spark; the scarred trail seemed to shake.

Tilth to filth.

CHAPTER 37

DISMISSED WITH PREJUDICE

Two weeks since the Tilt-Mine, the clay den unsealed,
They moved onto Free-Way, their bruises half-healed.

Leaf-Square swelled wider. "Breaking," Ink Crow now said,
Their steps froze in place, and the voices dropped dead.
"A slug from the quarry exposed what he knew,
Then vanished by dawn, leaving no trace or clue."

Starling breathed, "Witness protection, maybe now."
Wren shook his head: "Or a deep pit... you know how."

Ink Crow called to the crowd, "At first light they pried;
Wolves raided Grease Boar's vault; the ink barely dried.
On scrolls he had signed under government's guise,
He stripped Wild-Grove's life to finance his dark lies.
The wolves made the arrest with no need to speak.
The ledgers spelled guilt in a pattern too sleek.
His hoofprints were clear on each fraudulent deed:
No rumor nor hearsay, just motive and greed.

THE FOX WHO WONDERED WHY

Criminal counts are read at Knot-Hall today:
The docket's been called; watch what the judge will weigh."

Kit snapped, "We're going to see him stand in court."
Fox sighed, "I'll come along," no snarl, no retort.

Fox and Kit entered Knot-Hall's echoing maze;
Its arches bent shadows to smother their gaze.
The courtroom sat deep past ten doors and a bell,
Where verdicts were entered and truths dared to dwell.

Writ Vulture defended with feathery poise,
"The warrant was flawed in procedural noise.
There are state secrets; the proof must stay closed tight."
The judge bowed: "Without them, the case cannot bite."
The slug's sworn maps were kept, their true source unknown.
The facts had to be sealed, unexposed, not shown.

Next there came a defense tucked deep in the law;
It blessed *good-faith: harm*, for the *order* they saw.
It kept the mills turning and thawed city pipes,
Thus *public necessity* quelled all the gripes.

Verdict set aside, they struck a no-fault act,
And hired a court monitor, paid to redact.

Dismissed with Prejudice

No guilt was admitted; a fine skimmed the greed.
Workers kept caged, while the defendant was freed.
The vultures wore silk while the forest grew rot.
Their gavels were weapons; their mercy was bought.

The wolves held their ground as Grease Boar rose with pride;
His sentence erased, all the charges untied.
The files were sealed into lockers lined with brass,
While Wild-Grove's death, untried, was left to bypass.

Fox felt not a blaze, only vacancy's lee;
"Rules are for us," he thought, "exceptions for thee."

Bison grizzled out, "We witnessed what he stole!
He fenced off my kin from the watering hole!"
Clerk pressed the blotter, pretending a loud sneeze.
"Time's limited," she murmured, "Next matter, please."
The stenograph slate left her statement a dash:
Two lines deleted, then shoveled into ash.

Then Fox caught Shade Spider hunched in the back row,
A red file marked K-I-T, string-tied for show.
He breathed, "We must leave now," the warning kept small;
She read his face and they moved into the hall.

Storm Crow hit the wires with yet another dread,
"Urgent: A claw of panthers vows to shed red!"
Ink Crow snapped his quill; his pinions locked like wire.
He smeared the fresh headline, eyes narrowed to fire.

The scandal went quiet. The beasts turned away.
Grease Boar bought a vineyard and sang through the day.
No charges remained; no penalty was due.
Kit muttered, "It helps when the rules favor you."
When justice was murdered and laid in the street,
They passed out small mirrors to all they would meet.
A flicker, a like, and a shallow outrage,
That fits in your pocket and fits on one page.

They walked to Tilt-Mine, where the trees were plowed.
"When law bends for one," Fox judged, " it traps the crowd."
Kit whispered, "He did it and he walked away."
He said, "That's not justice. That's power at play."
Her gaze cut the mine where the last roots would be,
"What kind of law frees Grease Boar, yet still hunts me?"

Case law; caste law.

CHAPTER 38

THE PATTERN-WEB

The pines were draped in silk from the vast Web-Loom,
Where spiders read thoughts in a deep neural gloom.
Each tap of a paw, every turn of a phrase,
Was strung into strands that foretold creatures' days.

Kit crouched near a spruce with a question half-said,
But paused as a flicker spun over her head.
Ghost Spider descended with pitiless eyes,
"That query's forbidden; its pattern defies."
From shadow, Fox watched the great lattice of thread,
Where every cable pulsed in a networked spread.
Each fiber bore names in a flickering frame,
And Kit's tendril now flagged with an amber flame.

"You are marked for review," Ghost Spider pronounced,
"The network prosecutes the doubts you announced.
You once asked Great Owl what the Curtain concealed;
That signal was flagged, and your future was sealed."

Bluff Owl dropped from the dark with a soundless sway
With Kit's file: "Proceed! She has strayed from the way."

Then Scrub Snake arrived with a chrome-lidded tin:
Moss-Care's purple crystals that stilled Ringtail's grin.
He carefully measured out a single grain:
A spoon-tilt that promised compliance, not pain.

Three arbiters closed in, owl, spider, and snake,
To fix her tomorrow for the order's sake.

Fox gathered to spring, then the world turned to ice:
A clamp on his chest, an invisible vice.
He pressed to the earth till he blended with ground;
Eyes fixed and breath counted. Not even a sound.

They showed her a chart of her *Probable Ends,*
And outlined the branches where loyalty bends.

Bluff Owl tested, "Where is Fox? Speak now, say true."
Her vision went narrow; the woods lost their hue.

Ghost Spider twitched a line. The tag lights read *seen.*
Scrub Snake hissed, "Refuse, and we'll wipe your slate clean."

The Pattern-Web

We intercept early to keep you from breaks,
Correction begins when obedience shakes."

Her breath grew unsteady, her fur damp with dread,
While snake, spider, and owl edged close to her head.
"Be wise," hissed Ghost Spider, "with trails you pursue.
The web will not spare those who wander from view."

Owl's gaze was a hook. "Do you take back your word?"
"Yes," Kit replied, "it was folly and absurd."

Spider ran code through a radiant white wire,
But her vague words made the verdict a quagmire.

A humming node now woke on a yellow thread,
A cybernetic replied to what was said.
"The readings are faint, she might tilt from the fold,"
Kit's claws dug into dirt as her blood ran cold.

Owl weighed the answer: "We don't dose by choice.
But mercy betrayed will return with a voice."
Spider dimmed wires: "We spare her the web we bind;
Yet letting her slip leaves a debt in my mind."

Snake capped the tin: "Stand down. The proofs run thin still.
To drug what we doubt would rival our own will."
Bluff Owl faced Kit: "Walk straight, or sugar returns.
Another misstep, and your memory burns."

She swallowed her name till it tasted like shame;
The web left a welt where it edited blame.

"She's harmless," Owl murmured, and wheeled to the sky.
Ghost Spider withdrew; he let scanners run dry.
Scrub Snake sealed the tin and slithered off alone.
Kit trembled, breath stumbling, her claws cold as stone.

Fox stepped from the shadows, his voice thin and tight,
"You said the right words. It was wise to not fight."
He reached for her shoulder to loosen the snare;
She flinched from his paw, set her ears flat and bare.
The rope-burn from Grind-Bluff showed vivid and stark;
His shard-scarred paw rekindled her painful mark.

Kit sat in the glow of a half-broken strand,
Afraid of the thoughts she still held in her hand.
She folded her gaze like a page in low light;
The scar would keep speaking, an echo in white.

"They proclaimed I was wrong for asking too much."

Kit said, wiping ache from her palm with a touch.

Fox breathed, "We should flee. Free-Range buys us both room.

The forest has marked us; its verdict is doom.

We leave before sunrise and fade off the trail."

She nodded, "I'll go, though my courage is frail."

Pattern predicts; power constricts.

CHAPTER 39

FENCE OF BELIEF

Far down through the brambles with Kit at his heel,
Fox came to a field with a fence made of steel.
Within stood some creatures, serene in their stay;
The latch gaped wide open, but none walked away.

"Hello?" Fox called softly. "The path lies ahead."
Pig shook her head with a twitchy tilt and said,
"This pen is our shelter, our promise, our creed.
To step past its bounds is rebellion and greed.
I once slipped the gate on a night without moon;
Came back by dawn because freedom came too soon."

Kit blinked at the latch and tugged Fox by the sleeve.
Her voice filled with wonder, "Why don't they just leave?"
Her cadence held no scorn, just a puzzled tone,
The kind that can rattle what's set into stone.

Lamb near the barn gave a subdued, fleeting glance,
"They told us that freedom's a perilous chance.

Fence of Belief

Besides," he said quietly, "danger is near.
Free-Range gives us comfort. It is secure here."

"But who built the steel fence?" Fox asked with a frown.
"And why do you graze where the grass has turned brown?"
"The beavers designed it," Cow replied with ease.
"It works for us all. Please, no questions like these."

Pig stared at the hinge with her ears to the space,
Then looked at the meadow, then slipped back to place.
They stepped through the gate with no lock and no chain,
"This cage," Fox observed, "is the will you maintain."
"You speak like a rebel," Pig advised with dread.
"Your words bring us sorrow. They fill us with lead."

"Belief," Fox replied, "is a powerful thing.
It shapes each enclosure and softens the sting."
He touched the withered ground, once fervent and wild,
And thought of the laughter of his younger child.

Kit lingered to watch as the pen filled her view,
The beasts grazing at ease, the cloudless sky blue.
She followed behind Fox, weighed down by her doubt,
Glancing back to those who refused to walk out.

"They are safe," Fox said, "and perhaps they are wise.
There's warmth in the fortress belief sanctifies.
But the roads I must walk will not let me be,
I'll trade calm for truths that might set something free."

The wind moved the wheat like a half-written verse,
While Kit felt the weight of an internal curse.
"If faith makes us love what is done to our kind,"
She asked, "is the harshest cage built in our mind?"
The paddock fell silent; the hinge groaned with weight,
A slow, hollow creak from the mouth of the gate.

Fence your defense; your defense is a fence.

CHAPTER 40

TWO FLOCKS, ONE SHEAR

Fox and Kit pressed on through the Free-Range domain,
Where liberty's chorus still rattled its chain.
Behind them, the pens preached compliance as creed;
Ahead painted herds wore their virtue like greed.

In the grazing hills where the banners caught light,
Two flocks faced each other: one black and one white.
Their wool had been shorn, their colors now like charms.
Both swore the opposing side threatened their farms.

The white sheep wore feathers and sashes of blue,
And praised Cobalt Weasel as noble and true.
"We follow the voices that teach us to care,
And trust they'll bring justice if danger is there!"

The black sheep wore bark with a scarlet-toned crest.
They shouted for freedom and claimed to be blessed.
"Our chiefs speak of honor and paying the debts!
And Ruby Weasel guards us from overt threats!"

Each sheep scrolled devoutly on their Smart-Mirror,
Which showed them a world that was fractured by fear.
Their rage was reflected, refined, and made pure,
A system designed for the rich to endure.

The flocks had a shepherd, an anthem, one hymn;
Their chants rose so high that the heavens grew grim.
They clutched moral ground, yet grew red in the face
If asked who had drawn up the lines in their place.

Weasels made slick speeches from towers of stone,
Declaring that without them you stand alone.
They named every crisis on scrolls they prepared,
Then turned on their neighbors in fields that they shared.

Pearl Magpie slow-rolled crates to both camps for show,
The *SWEET-MILL* mark gleamed with the very same glow.
Mint Badger unbuckled the donors' twin case;
Two flocks bore *TILT-MINE's* presents, one purse per face.

Kit's laughter came brittle, like glass in the shade.
"Two edges," she murmured, "one merciless blade."

Below, the two masses marched circles in dust,
All certain their doctrine stood righteous and just.

Two Flocks, One Shear

But neither could see that the stage had been set,
By those who determine what sheep should forget.

Fox wandered between them with critical thought,
While slogans announced what the sides had been taught.
He asked both the herds on the edge of the glade,
"Aren't your weasels' two flags in the same parade?"

"Deceiver!" cried white sheep. "You march with the red!"
"Blue-traitor!" the black sheep with equal rage said.

They turned on him sharply with venom and spite,
"Don't poison the young one's mind from what is right!"

Kit stepped into view, her fur bristling and tall:
"He listens, not lies; he just questions it all.
Truth isn't a color, and doubt isn't fear,
And you can't claim honor while deaf to what's near."

They climbed up a knoll to let tensions subside,
Then Fox spoke with stress of a fact long denied:
"They filter out proof if it weakens their song,
For they'd rather belong than admit they were wrong.
Weasels weaponized hope into groups that fight,
Then turned every shadow to cover their might.

They draft cunning laws built to herd and delay,
Then they feed flocks cues just to profit and stay."

He paused briefly, then his voice cut like a knife,
"They twist falsehoods in your mind and steal your life.
Your love and your hate are both bought and arranged;
You think you're awake, but your cage hasn't changed."

Kit leaned into Fox as the twilight grew wide,
"They'd welcome us back if we just pick a side.
If asking for more means we walk on our own,
Then truth is my compass, a guiding touchstone."

Chants diverge; coffers converge.

CHAPTER 41

THE PUPPET KING

Fox and Kit heard drums as the wind split their ears,
From beyond the fence came a chorus of cheers.
"Revolt!" cried the wind. "They're demanding their say!"
So they walked the Free-Way that led to the fray.

Leaf-Square was seething; the animals stood tall:
Banners flew above the sycamore Ear-Hall.
From lofty poles, hairline cables had been hung;
They parted the blue sky and sharpened its tongue.

"Bring down the Thirteen!" bellowed Ferret with pride.
"This time, we rise and we will not be denied!"

He roared on a stump with a crown on his brow,
His voice like a drum and his paw like a plow.
"They take far too much; they steal away our breath!
We demand fresh fruit or they'll bargain with death!"

Ravens scattered streamers and lights from the trees,
And piped in a jingle designed to appease.
"We will double the feasts and triple the play.
No more troubling choices to ruin your day!"

Raccoon dogs observed the mob with rules in tow,
Policing the glee so it wouldn't outgrow.
They flashed paper placards to shepherd the grin,
And trimmed every murmur that threatened the win.

The mob roared approval, so tidy, so bright,
While Fox watched them dance in manufactured light.
"They rally for release," he said with a frown,
"Yet no one here asks who forged the golden crown."

"Pecans and huckleberries for us!" chirped Jay.
Kit noticed fine wires where new slogans would play.
In the thistle's shadow, she saw a faint gleam:
Subtle silver strings pulling Ferret's regime.

The guiding threads vanished through trees far away,
Where a mirrored tower caught bits of the day.
Great Owl bent backward with a word and a twitch,
Governing the march with a gear and a switch.

The Puppet King

He toggled the catchwords, rewrote the demands,
And Ferret adjusted with supporting hands.
Owl studied the motions, the switches in code,
Each pivot then shifted to follow that mode.

"Funnel to the square! Let the oil braziers burn!
But not toward the vaults; let's not crash or churn.
Let's celebrate freedom with pastries and song!
Let us rave for new life, not dwell on the wrong!"

Fox glanced toward the wires, his breath drawn in slow,
"They're watching us. I think they already know."
He then spoke calmly, though the slogans still sting,
"No ruler stands tall when he's a puppet king.
They've softened the chains, but the binding remains,
Just cushioned in laughter and glittery gains."

Kit leaned into Fox as the music gained speed,
"This isn't a movement; it's staged to proceed."
He felt it as well, eyes combing the whole crowd,
The weighted intent of a watcher's soft shroud.

They sat in a field where the sky remained wide,
And weighed the noise that no remark could yet hide.

"Even liberty," Kit added, her voice very clear,
"Can serve as a leash dressed in comfort and cheer."

Fox pulled her close as the false freedom bells rang,
And over the rooftops the creatures all sang.
"If liberty leads from the end of a string,
What truth can be found in the songs that they sing?"

Puppet rights; puppeteer writes.

CHAPTER 42

BEYOND THE CURTAIN

Breakfast was quiet, no banners, no refrain:
Just berries and tea during a cooling rain.
Kit breathed, "There's nothing here for us anymore.
I want to see what's beyond the Curtain's door."

Fox flinched northward, toward the veil's hidden seam.
"I don't know," he replied with low self-esteem.
He balked at the thought and the weight of his fate.
"Think of the fence," Kit urged. "Pig choosing to wait."
Fox felt his shard-scar prickle, glanced up in dread,
"I'll follow you to the end," he firmly said.

Kit led Fox past Owl-Spire to the Cross-Track's path;
The hike felt tense from the fear of Great Owl's wrath.
Beyond stood the Curtain, stitched tight with old lies,
And past it, the unknown underneath dark skies.

They stepped through the shimmer, its threads falling slack,
Each pace left behind what had clung to their back.

Their breath slowed to stillness, the moment held tight,
They crossed into real and abandoned the fright.

The air tasted verdant, like mint crushed and clean;
Cool soil kissed their pads with a soft, earthen sheen.
No fences, no wardens, no ledgers or locks,
Only flowers blooming next to mossy rocks.

The vines bore ripe fruit in the bend of the trees,
And mushrooms flourished in the blow of the breeze.
No coins in the clover, no lies in the loam,
Just living and being in a place called home.

Pronghorn and Cougar shared a meal side by side,
With no badge of rank, and no shame to divide.
They passed Antelope who painted rocks with clay,
Her hooves smeared with colors the wind couldn't sway.

Muskox gathered strawberries out of the frost,
Smiling although many had withered and lost.
Her cheer wasn't measured in speed or in gain;
It rose from the tending, not from a locked chain.

"What is this place?" Fox whispered in profound awe.
"A myth left behind? A forest without law?"

Turtle then chuckled from underneath green ferns.
"No, we call it True-Glen, which always returns.
I walked to the woods after reading a tale,
That I hid at Mind-Stump and then crossed the veil.
I gave to the soil what was meant for the sky,
I carried the story so it would not die."

"You buried that fable?" Kit's eyes opened wide.
"A thorn found my hide where your secret would hide.
I tucked it away and slipped past their decree;
Your hidden seed sprouted and started in me."

He turned toward Kit with a wise, patient croon,
"You kept its ember. I had hoped it would swoon."
"Freedom," stated Turtle, "isn't always sweet.
We stumble, we mend, we know loss in defeat.
There's laughter and song, but also the harsh ache.
For even in ease, every heart can still break.
We quarrel and then learn; we build and we blend.
We falter, forgive; we then learn and transcend.
But here we feel wholly our sorrow, our bliss,
And nothing trades away the raw truth of this."

Fox touched the tilled soil where the wild onions grew;
Kit knelt right beside him, drinking in the view.

Not thrills from a stream, nor escape from a creed,
But the hush of a moment that fed their need.
His nerves matched the creek in a slow, even glide;
Not only denied, something living supplied.

"How has this endured so long?" Fox wondered why.
Turtle replied, "We plant where others won't try.
We refused the pleasures that come with a cost,
And chose honest labor over comfort lost."

They sat in the grass where the cool waters fell,
And tasted a world that had broken the spell.
Kit whispered to Turtle, her voice warm but shy,
"Is joy what you grow, not just something you buy?"

Turtle responded to Kit's astounded gaze,
"It's labor of tending through shadow and phase.
It comes from connection, from feeling things through;
From dancing with sorrow, and letting joy brew."

Turtle grinned happily, and offered them root.
"It's bitter, but cleanses. We call it True-Fruit."
The tuber bit, and rich soil clung to its skin;
They knew they had tasted where sound things begin.

Then Turtle cupped water and breathed: "Gather round!
Four pours in this order: the gone, self, friend, ground.
Pour first for the dead; let the river recall.
Sip second for yourself, to steady us all.
Share third with a friend till your shoulders release;
The last to the earth, so the circle keeps peace."

Kit traced every motion, each pour, pause, and set:
A ritual pattern she would not forget.
She brushed back the dust from a stone carved with care,
"They guarded this place while others didn't dare."
"You kept this," said Turtle, "I know by your tune."
She felt herself belong, her heart in commune.

Fox gazed at the light with resolve in his frame,
"If life can flourish here, why not spread the flame?"
With True-Fruit and rites folded close like a seed,
They turned back through the Curtain to sow their need.

Eden is seeded; not ceded.

CHAPTER 43

VOICE OF FLAME

A windstorm was nearby, clouds swirled in the air;
The revolution failed inside of Leaf-Square.
Kit followed Fox, who had embers in his eyes.
He could not endure the continuous lies.

"You are my future," Fox said under the storm,
"You were not made to fit in their perfect form."
He pulled Kit closer with the rain drawing near,
"But you are the reason I won't kneel to fear.
I have no great riches, no kingdom, no crest,
Just poems and shards embedded in my chest."

He kissed her forehead, then turned toward the square
To conquer deceit with no shield or prayer.

Kit watched from the hedgerow; rain silvered her eyes.
He glanced at the courtyard where they told their lies.
She fled through the woodlands, her breath sharp and fast,
As he marched to the square to expose the past.

Voice of Flame

He'd wandered through shadows, through silence and screams,
And now he returned with the weight of his dreams.

The creatures assembled in cautious array,
While Great Owl took place in the time-honored way.

"The forest is stable," he hooted on high.
"Each animal has learned not to question why."
The air crackled thick with unspoken decree;
To speak was to risk both his place and his tree.

But the fire in Fox, banked season by season,
Now burned with a purpose that consumed reason.
He cleared his throat as the masses thickened deep,
To expose what is real and was buried in sleep.

"Everything is a lie!" Fox howled, flames in breath.
"You sold us deceit while preparing our death.
You named the Curtain safety, a holy wall,
But wove it to blind us, not guard us at all.
You drafted our choices before we could choose;
Then priced out the water and called it good news.
You inked us in ledgers and called them our names,
And taught us to fear the small ember that flames.

O owl, you preach order from vellum and stone,
But gagging the living is mere rule alone.
You traded our berries for glitter and ache;
Sweet fog for the hunger true fruits used to wake.
You sold us our daylight and named it a wage;
Then rented our shelters and tightened the cage.
Is Starling's bare doorway your vaunted relief?
Are Otter's cold pups the cost of your belief?
You blurred Ringtail's memory, trimmed back his song,
And labeled it mercy for thinking too long.
Is Possum's death still *'procedure'* in your law?
He offered a flower; the wolves claimed a claw.
You minted obedience, gold on a tree,
Then taught us to beg while you rationed the sea.
You arranged our revolts with your wires and screens,
Then sold us their echoes as liberty's scenes.
You twisted the rules to a bright, bloodless ring,
A halo you polish to crown the same king.
You tracked every whisper, and charged it as wealth;
You promised us safety and totaled our health.
This wasn't a shield; it hid beneath a veil:
A garden turned stage so your tallies prevail.

Wise Great Owl, your *'order'* is fear with a mask;
Your *'wisdom'* a script that forbids us to ask.

Voice of Flame

Your book bound our futures in roles we were not,
Then left us the blanks where we mend the old plot.
At Rush-Dam you strangled the river's great flow;
At Sweet-Mill you sugared our sickness to glow.
You split us in colors and trained us to fight;
Two edges, one weapon, both false and both bright.
Your Pattern-Web stalked us with numbers for fate,
And guessed at our crimes so the cuffs needn't wait.
Your quiet handshakes made the Wild-Grove a pit;
And Knot-Hall washed it clean while the stumps still sit.
Is Cardinal's seized pouch your balance made plain?
Are skunks penned inside Safe-Patch your new campaign?
You call it protection; I call it a stage,
The puppet king's chorus reciting your page.
Look down at your claws. Do their stories agree?
Or do your own scars contradict what you see?
Let silence be tinder, not muzzle or oath;
Let questions be fire that harvests the new growth.
If embers must fall, let them burn through the chain,
Not truth, but the leash that parades as our gain.
The Curtain's not shelter; it shears out your sight:
It darkened our eyes while your ledgers wrote night.
Choose roots over ribbons; step out of their play.
Begin with a why and let daylight have say."

THE FOX WHO WONDERED WHY

Sly Weasel stood up with a twitch of her lip,
And motioned Slate Wolf with a firm-fingered grip.
"The order is fragile," she growled through a glare.
"Keep quiet, or vanish, We won't even care.
So sit down and shut up. You're stirring the pot.
Your facts are unhelpful; your tales are a blot."

Murmurs grew jagged, and the air held its breath.
For speaking dissent risks immediate death.

Alpha Wolf near the gate gave a snarling growl:
One twitch from Fox and he'd strike without a howl.
Then Slate Wolf raised muzzle to rain-cooled metal;
The storm on her tongue rang hard as a kettle.

Owl gave a signal and the Pattern-Web stirred,
Predicting which voices would soon be unheard.

"The garden can flourish," said Fox with a cry,
"But lies in the roots make the harvest go dry.
If we trade our silence for comfort and ease,
Then real rots in cages while flatterers please."

"He mocks our foundations," Great Owl boomed aloud.
"He poisons the minds gathering in this crowd.

He threatens the design with riddles and flame.
This isn't wisdom; it's a dangerous game."

He flared out his wings and intoned with great care,
"This Fox is a hazard, a spark we can't spare.
He questions the trust that we've all built so long.
His thoughts are misguided; his thinking is wrong."

"Perhaps," Fox replied, "but if embers must fall,
Let it burn what binds us, not facts most of all.
A fire that reveals is a flame I'll defend,
Though it leaves me alone and costs me my den.
Truth doesn't shout; it begins with a small stir:
Lean close to the quiet and you'll feel its spur."

His words lit the hush like a torch in the dark,
And some turned away while others felt a spark.
Marmot in the rear felt his whiskers tingle:
A chime in his chest like a winter jingle.

The wolves bared their sharp teeth, but Fox did not shake;
For silence, when purchased, is always a fake.

"Now!" thundered Sly Weasel. "This treason won't stand!"
The wolves closed around him with shackles in hand.

A truncheon came down with a crack and a thud;
Fox tasted the pennies; his mouth filled with blood.

They slung him on planks in a clattering dray;
The wheels bit the ruts and ground mud into clay.
Slate Wolf looked at him with a softening brow;
Her duty went weightless, then hardened in vow.

Oriole, angered, let loose a piercing call,
And each guard's gaze swung toward him on the wall.
Starling stooped sudden with a shiv cut from tin,
And severed the reins at the buckle and pin.
Cardinal flashed crimson and battered the hood;
The draft-team reared backward and planted in wood.

Ringtail slid underneath the axle's low rim,
Picked open the hasp with a bent copper shim.
The tailboard released with a grunt and a groan.
"Get out!" Ringtail hissed. "Take the bramble alone."

Plumb Beaver lunged out, but she fumbled the gate;
Her paw missed the locking latch, one breath too late.
Fox slipped through the briars and swallowed the rain;
The blood on his tongue matched the storm on the plain.

Voice of Flame

Back at the watch-post, Shade Spider balled her fist,
And scored *FOX* and *KIT* on the *Most Wanted* list.

Back in the brambles with his breath turning thin,
No torchbearers left, just the dark drawing in.
But in his head returned the voice he first heard:
Is the truth worth telling if none heed the word?

Name the lie; say goodbye.

CHAPTER 44

CHOOSING THE SHARD

That night in the thicket where shadows ran deep,
Fox curled in a hollow and drifted to sleep.
But dreams are not gentle to those who have seen;
They pull at the seam of the stories kept clean.

He wandered through mists in a forest once known,
Where berries were sweet and the rules overgrown.
The voice from the past called him back to the old:
It's safer here, Fox. Let the harsh truth grow cold.

The den reappeared, warm, unbroken, and neat,
With solace and memory curled at his feet.
The walls held a trace of pine sap and black tea,
And every soft blanket sighed, "You are still free."

The hearth offered fire with its cinnamon glow,
Where endings felt certain and time had moved slow.
Porcupine poured coffee and told fairy tales,
Careful to skip the mirrors, masters, and scales.

Choosing the Shard

Fox flexed the old cut where the shard made its mark;
The comfort went rigid, too spotless, too stark.

"Forget all you've gathered," Porcupine then grinned.
"The questions just wear you and forget you sinned.
We missed you, but your defiance made us frown.
Rest now, dear Fox. Lay your allegories down."

He almost curled deep where the floor was well-swept,
But brittle, faint odors betrayed how it kept.
It carried the tang of a sanitized class:
The same tidy order that cut him with glass.

The pillows drew closer, the heat pressed in tight,
The scent of the past almost drowned out the fight.
A line shone beneath him, thin, amber and long;
It hummed in a cadence both eerie and strong.

"What is this roadway?" Fox inquired through the haze.
"A thorn or escape from the havens I praise?"
The den fell away as the fog turned to ash,
Then thundered around him like memory's lash.
"The path I have chosen is narrow and steep.
Each truth that I touched made my soul howl and creep."

Then one crystal shard pierced the pad of his paw.
Not punishment, no, more a moment of awe.
It burned like her voice when Kit asked him, "But why?"
And answers rained out from the ache of his cry.

The sting was a promise he could not release:
A wound that cuts lies is the start of true peace.
He followed the thread through the roots of the night,
Bleeding but fearless without the need of light.

"To know, then forget, is a cushion too thin.
I'll carry the wound, but I won't go back in."
The night turned to dawn as he opened his eyes,
Kit's questions were like flames that seared right through lies.
"For her life, I will bleed. For her, I will burn.
But if I do not speak, will the flame return?"

Illusion sews; truth tears.

CHAPTER 45

THE QUESTION AT THE BRINK

The fire had faltered and the stillness grew wide.
Fox left the hollow, but felt shadows inside.
Was Kit up ahead, or already behind?
The trail came apart like loose threads in his mind.

He sat on a stone with his head in his paws,
No banner to carry, no just or great cause.
"What if," he murmured, "my dissent came too late,
And no one remembers what sparked this self-hate?"
The doubts he had seeded were lost in the breeze,
And hearts once awakened had turned back to ease.
Some called him a traitor who ruptured their calm,
For truth is a sun that outshines any psalm.

He crumpled in silence, no strength left to feign,
His body was unbroken, burdened with pain.
What if I've become the one I swore to fight?
He looked to the stars, but they offered no light.

His lungs worked in fragments, his chest barely stirred.
His thoughts curled in corners where nothing was heard.
Had seasons of turmoil, of questions and cries,
Led only to ashes beneath shadowed skies?

He reached Grind-Bluff's brink, saw the void, deep and sheer.
"*One step,*" his mind said, "*Let's finish it right here.*"
The wind tipped him right to the edge of the wall.
The dark voice said, "*Step once, and it settles all.*"

Then Kit's memory crossed the distance like rope
and caught where his air had let go of its hope.
He fell to the earth, ugly sobs, ragged breath;
Her face in his mind pulled him back from that death.

He rose without triumph, no meaning, no cheer,
Only one measured step had carried him here.
Then softly it came, not a voice, but a hum,
From deep in the dirt where the quiet ones drum.
No chorus was sung, no melody was played;
But something still listened each time that he prayed.

A single green shoot curled slowly up from the clay,
Not bold, not heroic, but still finding its way.

The Question at the Brink

He watched in the calm, where his hope had been thin.
The ember still lives as it flickers within.

He stood with no victory, no smile, no word;
One small resolve returned to where he had stirred.

Far down the dark path where the moonlight withdrew,
Kit kindled a spark as she stepped into view.

No banners were lifted, no battles were won,
But something endured when the aching was done.
Two figures drew closer, both blistered yet true,
And warmth shaped itself in the space between two.

She whispered, "We've given all that we can spare."
He answered, "The price paid is proof that we care."
Her voice trembled low as the cold drifted through,
"What if the courage means I'm losing you, too?"

He murmured, "I wavered. I almost turned back.
I nearly chose silence to cover my track.
I feared you would fade while the shouting burned bright;
I stood at the brink and I swallowed the light."

She answered, "I fear you'll be taken from me;
Yet running from truth I refuse to decree."

She loosened her wool blanket, ash-gray and frayed;
She drew it around, and their heartbeats obeyed.
The night kept its cold, yet it loosened its teeth;
Two pulses made shelter, a small glow beneath.

Remember the ember.

CHAPTER 46

CIRCLE OF EARS

By moonlight, the forest lay dreaming in sleep,
Yet something had stirred in the heart of its deep.
A tremor of order fell out of its place,
As though the dark loosened the knots of its lace.
Fox padded through grassland with Kit at his side:
Two shadows that traversed with questions inside.
They halted before a faint shimmer of light
That pooled in a hollow and gentled the night.

A circle of creatures sat in a small nook,
Beside the shoreline of the tranquil Hush-Brook.
No banners, no badges, no titles to bear;
Plain questions rose softly, like seeds through the air.

"I heard," murmured Mouse, "that Gold-Leaves aren't the source,
That water runs free without bridle or force."
"I saw," said Doe, "that the watchers all have ties,
And they too are bound by the power they prize."

"I dreamed," said Pheasant, "of a garden unbound,
Where no voice decides how another is crowned."

Fox lingered outside, unsure if he belonged,
Till Marmot's small tone uttered words Fox had longed:
"A fox once said something that stuck in my fur:
That truth doesn't shout; it begins as a stir."

The gathering stilled, then it parted with grace,
And Fox stepped within, feeling time slow its pace.
"You... heard what I said?" His words carried slight doubt.
"Not all," Marmot smiled. "Just enough to seek out."

"We're not here to follow," said Doe with a nod.
"We've come here to wonder, to turn over sod.
No need for a crown to declare what is flame,
True hearts that remember, and eyes that reclaim."
The stillness that followed was steady and clear,
Not hollow, but heavy, with power to hear.

Then Kit stood, her tone neither timid nor loud,
Yet it rolled through them like a wind through a cloud.
"We've all felt the chain, its jostle and its weight.
But knowing is nothing if we choose our fate.

Circle of Ears

You gathered to listen; now rise and be more.
The Curtain still stands, but we've seen what's in store.
If truth is the seed, then the step is the rain;
It's time to move forward, or sit here in vain."

She lifted a bowl from the creek's even flow;
The moon wrote a ribbon of tremulous glow.
She tilted the dish till the stream said dead names;
She sipped for her own life to steady her flames.
She passed to a neighbor till tightness would cease;
The last kissed the roots for the keeping of peace.

Fox watched as she filled the vessel to the brim:
Rope-burns worn like bracelets, old scars, stark and slim.
He let go of guarding; his ego went small.
He stood as her equal and answered her call.

The circle rose slowly, no shouting, no drums,
Mere footsteps through grass where the low night hums.
They knew that the road might be riddled with cost,
But the fire in Kit meant they'd never be lost.

Before first dawn, the circle unlaced its ring;
Packs shouldered the long calm; clean waters would sing.

THE FOX WHO WONDERED WHY

Kit lingered with Fox by the creek-braided reed;
Her paw on the bowl, his eyes finally freed.

"I'm taking them west," she said, voice calm as tide.
"What if I fail them, Fox? What if I misguide?"
"You won't keep them safe," he replied, warm and plain.
"You'll keep them awake: that's safer than a chain."

"And you?" she asked. "If the darkness hunts your track?"
He smiled. "It tried once and I found my will back.
At Grind-Bluff's outcrop you tied me to the ground;
I've nothing to prove now, with roads to be found."

"I want you beside me," she breathed, half a plea.
"If I walk at your elbow, you'll lean on me.
Your fire keeps seasons; it does not need a guard.
I'd only make simple what must remain hard."

She frowned, then she softened. "Will you eat and sleep?"
"I'll eat what is honest, and keep what we keep.
When dusk presses inward, I pour to keep worth
For the lost, the living, a friend, lastly earth."

She pressed her brow to his. "If I call, come near."
He answered, "I'll be there before you can fear."

Circle of Ears

They laughed through the ache as the dawn split in two.
"Go lead them," he said, "all I learned came from you."

Kit turned to the west with a steadier stride;
Fox tipped two claws upward and stepped to the side.
Not broken, not lost, just given their free will:
Two paths from one ember, both burning there still.

Leaders listen; listeners lead.

CHAPTER 47

FOUND AND FOUNDED

Six moons have waned since the circle of ears broke;
Fox walked out his sorrow till there wasn't smoke.
A warm gust had laid a compass to his breast;
Then he followed the sunset and headed west.

In shadows which wolves had long ceased to patrol,
A garden grew wide like the core of a soul.
He followed a scent through the thorn and the sand
To a petrified reef within public land.

Fox found a sign carved in driftwood named *New-Glen*,
Kit's paw in the letters, the curve of her pen.

The reef and the creek conserved the True-Glen's light,
Then something forgotten stepped back into sight.
Marmot stacked wood bowls where the warm loaves would steam.
Mouse fastened the twine for a food-trading scheme.

Found and Founded

Doe hauled buckets of water for the whole clan.
Otter placed levees where the side-current ran.
Pig stitched warm quilts that had a copper-soft glow.
Ringtail guarded the edge where he could lie low.

Ahead, Kit taught Pup how to strike a fair deal,
Turning grains to chorus, a loaf to a meal.
"Isn't this dangerous?" asked Pup with a blink.
"It is," she replied, "but we live on the brink."

Fox stepped from the bracken; she burst into tears.
Next laughter broke through them and flattened their fears.
Their foreheads met; the months fell off like thawed frost.
"I thought the worst," cried Kit. "I believed you'd lost."
"I kept your name," he replied, "each trail and track."
"Please keep it," she smiled. "Do not ever go back."

"You carried the will of True-Glen," he said small.
"I will not leave you; I found peace through it all."
He knelt by the stream, tracing spirals in clay,
A haven where voices could speak without sway.

Then two shouts flared bright at the seed-weighing stand;
Squirrel claimed his share with the beans in Wren's hand.

Kit raised a calm paw: "Let portions match the need.
We scatter, we save, we share; make sport of greed."

She spread drying kernels in cool creekside shade.
"Hold thirds for the future from the fruit we've made.
Mark the location; keep them cool, dark, and sealed.
Let hunger choose first, then the future is healed.
Store three from each basket, one eaten, one freed,
Last buried for winter: the covenant seed.
No center to worship," she said to the ring.
"Make paws be the law and the seasons our king."

Bullfrog stepped forward; his melody then rolled;
The harmony, once off-key, had returned bold.
Peace-River, the chorus, a calm running tune:
It braided the breaths like a slow-rising moon.

Goldfinch joined in the song the Leaf-Dome had banned,
Softening the grass in the dry, bitter sand.
Starling wove harmony, Cardinal sang lead;
Fox heard the music and embraced the slow speed.

They laid meadow flowers onto Possum's shrine.
Chrysanthemum marked what words couldn't define.

Found and Founded

He ladled out stew of wild onion and leek;

Then ate without speaking, each swallow grew meek.

As now the tune circled from ember to eave,

He hummed it to himself, unwilling to leave.

The stories went still like a page never turned;

Power had uncoiled from the talons that burned.

Kit murmured to Pup in the green of the glade:

"True freedom runs deep and it never will fade."

No slogans, no flags, no decree to defend,

Only herbs in a bin, a coat from a friend.

No signals were raised, no revolt to avow,

Just words never repeated, and none asked how.

The dread was not gone. It had softened its teeth,

And hope bloomed in footsteps still planting beneath.

Fox turned to find Kit by the stream's silver sheen,

Then asked, "Will you let this place remain unseen?"

The Mint-Tree stood bare, with no paw left to bribe;

For hunger now bowed to the hearth and the tribe.

The halls of exchange stood abandoned and worn;

No animals queued up, no tallies were sworn.

"What sparked this collapse?" Great Owl called from the spire.

Shade Spider replied, "They have no more desire.

The demand has lessened for candy and bread.

Fewer work for Gold-Leaves; our power is dead."

Tend the tending, not to tender.

CHAPTER 48

THE CURTAIN RETURNS

A hush gripped New-Glen as a shimmer unfurled;
A Curtain descended to split half their world.
Not fabric nor thread, but a veil of unseen,
That flickered like dream-light through shadows and green.

Brass trumpets of thunder rolled down from the hill,
And Great Owl appeared, cloaked in velvet and will.

The beavers built quickly with levels and twine,
A lattice of pulleys, exact by design.
Arch Beaver called measures, squared timber to span;
He wrenched each block-line and set braces to plan.
Plumb Beaver checked rigging with resin-stained hand,
Her eyes flicked towards Kit, then back on command.

The ropes sang like saw-teeth, the blocks cinched up tight;
Each wheel bit the sunlight and sliced it to white.
They hammered and hoisted, they tightened the seams
To anchor old myths in mechanical dreams.

A stage rose from timbers with smoke curling high,
And stories were painted to darken the sky.

"Return," Great Owl called, "to the order you knew.
The balance has been broken. The wild bleeds through."

From behind his broad pinions, Bluff Owl peered down;
The parchment unrolled as she managed a frown.
Slate Wolf kept formation, yet widened a seam;
A gap in the cordon that let in a beam.

"Without our lead," cried Great Owl, "the stars go black.
The forest will crumble. No truth will come back."
Crows wheeled above them in a fanfare of pride,
Scattering feathers from verses they supplied.
Storm Crow lit the headline to varnish the sky;
Ink Crow lowered his quill and let it go dry.
"Behold!" they proclaimed with theatrical glee,
"Great Owl has returned! Now rejoice and agree!"

Grease Boar rolled in barrels to butter the rails;
Hedge Boar kicked chocks to let the slope end the tales.
Kinder Goat called roll for the lesson of fear;
Rove Goat drafted questions and opened each ear.

The Curtain Returns

Bronze Badger, once banker, now served as a clerk;
Mint Badger snapped, "Stamp now!" Bronze refused the work.
Fat Rat hissed, "Hold stock!" to the ship and the sea;
Dock Rat broke fellowship, "Eat now and be free."

Now Kit stepped forward, her timbre cutting clean:
"This display's the same as the last one we've seen.
Your balance is built on the fears you invent;
We've walked without you and the forest still bent."
From the stage Masked Weasel unsealed a decree,
And halted, wax cooling calmly at his knee.

Fox watched, astonished, as courage took her frame.
Kit, whom he had guarded, now carried the flame.
Writ Vulture kept talons on fines he could reap
As Plea Vulture let papers drop into deep.
Balm Snake raised sweet vials to quiet the doubt;
Scrub Snake turned to the roots and poured them all out.

Kit turned to the crowd, her words precise but kind,
"You've seen our glen blossom where no leash could bind.
They measured your acclaim, they filtered your cries,
They handed you cages disguised as the skies.
Step past their illusions, don't cling to their stage.
The Curtain's no wall, just a fence to encage."

She reached for the halyard and her claws felt strange.
She paused like Pig stuck inside the fenced Free-Range.
Slate Wolf shifted weight and left room in the ring.
Alpha Wolf roared for ranks, no one did a thing.
Kit trembled, she squared with a breath, steady-slow,
And dropped the main pulley, "We don't need this show."

The Thirteen had froze at her sudden command.
Plumb Beaver let go, each rope fell as it fanned.
Shade Spider tuned threads, tagged those who were misplaced.
Ghost Spider struck, the Pattern-Web was erased.
The pulley hit hard with a bone-deep, bare thwack;
No creature looked back when they heard the loud smack.
They fixed on each other as the grandstand fell,
And held one another to break the old spell.

Fox heard the dull thud like Frog's jar in his head,
Yet kept his gaze level on faces instead.
He let the show fall without tracking its arc;
A small, certain smile warmed the rim of his dark.
Pearl Magpie clutched glitter to dam the daylight;
As Gilt Magpie dropped his Gold-Leaves out of sight.

One by one, creatures blinked hard and stepped away,
To a place where the Curtain's reign could not sway.

The Curtain Returns

The veil fell apart with a whisper, not roar;
Its edges dissolved into dust on the floor.

No battle was fought, no horn needed to blow,
Just hearts that stayed open, and minds that would know.

Great Owl's feathers dulled as his costume wore thin,
And sunlight broke clean through the stage behind him.
Bluff Owl let the parchment unroll to her feet;
She watched the sunshine climb and chose not to cheat.

The forest held still, though its pulse didn't shake
As dawn carved a pathway no shadow could take.
Now symbols felt weightless, like gauze in the light;
The Curtain lost purpose when hearts walked from fright.

By the stream's rapids where the waters ran fast,
Kit stood spent, eyes fixed on the flow rushing past.
She turned to the beasts with a voice calm and sure:
"Someday, they'll return. Be ready to endure."

Feed the real; starve the reel.

CHAPTER 49

THE FLAME THAT LISTENS

New-Glen was peaceful in a late-golden light,
Its field now clear, no longer blurred by the fight.
No crowns had been taken, no flag had been raised:
Only gates left open and creatures amazed.

Kit stood at the heart of the clearing's wide span,
Her paw on the log like a map for a plan.
The young ones drew near with their questions held high,
"What now?" they asked her. "Do we build, or just try?"

"We lead by the tending," she said without pause,
"Not ruling with thrones or creating new laws.
We guard each small voice and we watch where they fade.
We mend what was broken, not what had been made."
She taught the four pours at the creekside's wide berth:
"First for death, self, and friends; the last one for earth.
No keeping of secrets," she smiled in the light.
"What mends must be common, or else it turns blight."

Fox rested beside the embers' low-lit gleam;
A slow, steady glow like the hush of a dream.
He stirred them to life, his words careful, austere:
"Kit plants what will grow. You must guard it from fear.
Ask more than you answer, let doubt be your guide,
For comfort can cost what your questions provide.
Yet truth is not thunder: it seldom does shout,
But waits in the silence where power fades out."
Fox shifted the benches back down from a tier,
Leveled all the stumps so no *high seat* was near.

Kit saw Gilt Magpie slip some kernels aside;
One glance, he returned them, his feathers showed pride.
Bluff Owl set her pencil down; she chose to hear.
Ink Crow cleaned his lenses; he printed it clear.
Slate Wolf eased the cordon; she let mercy in.
Scrub Snake sealed the flasks; to let healing begin.
Ghost Spider stopped scanning; he slackened his web.
Plumb Beaver loosed rigging; she eased rafters' ebb.
Rove Goat burned old rubrics; he opened the field.
Hedge Boar shelved her memos; she let reasons yield.
Bronze Badger dropped ledgers; she denied the rate.
Masked Weasel spoke honestly; he held the gate.
Plea Vulture dropped motions; she spoke for the meek.
Dock Rat shared the profits; she nurtured the weak.

Then Crane stepped up, his talons tipped in the gold,
"What if truth darkens, or the stories grow cold?"
Kit met his soft gaze with a steadying fire,
"Then light them up again, even if you tire."

The flame crackled low as the night took its place,
And creatures leaned close, felt its warming grace.
No banners were lifted, no titles were worn;
Yet deep in the dark, a foundation was sworn.

Fox rose without glory, his eyes on the sky.
"Worry wears soft masks; remember to ask '*Why?*'
While even one voice dares to stand and draw near,
The Curtain will fade when the flame renders clear."

Kit's gaze swept the clearing, her stance firm and sure.
"This isn't ending; it's more work to endure.
If the dark comes again, we'll meet it awake
And keep what we've sprouted for the truth's own sake."

No chair; all share.

CHAPTER 50

THE ANSWERING SILENCE

Fox wandered alone where no questions could stir
Past language and law, past the brushstroke of fur.
Night watchers were absent, no banners, no crowd,
Just mist in the hollows and trees leaning proud.

He came to a gorge where the flowers grew thin;
No sign bade him enter, yet welcomed him in.
A stone lay unmarked in the cool of the shade;
Its face bore no edict, no script that forbade.

A light rain arrived, tasting fern, root, and stone;
It braided the dust to a skin of its own.
His limbs bore the weight of long-traveled terrain,
Each step carved by struggle, by sorrow, by strain.

The shard had not killed him, but left what it taught:
That peace without cost is the comfort that's bought.
He sat without reason, no lesson to teach,
No purpose to proclaim, no summit to reach.

THE FOX WHO WONDERED WHY

For truth, he now knew, was not always a flame;
It lived in the quiet that asked for no name.
He held for a minute, each breath calm and still;
And silence grew wider, a room time could fill.

The wind didn't argue, the brook didn't plead;
The moss kept its counsel but gave what he'd need.
He moved with the trees, and they answered in kind:
Not words, only rhythm that softens the mind.

Kit padded near him with no fear in her tread.
She asked him no questions, nor future to dread.
She curled under his shadow, then blinked and yawned.
But Fox only nodded: no lesson had dawned.
Her paws bore old rope-burns gone pale in the dew;
They mattered like seasons the forest once knew.
For somewhere far past the revolt and the roar,
Outside each question that had opened a door,
There dwelled a soft knowing, a root without sound,
That only grows deeper the less it is found.

Fox did not depart, and he did not arrive.
He simply was present, awake, and alive.
And in that still moment, unmeasured by time,
He heard the Earth answer with a subtle chime.

The Answering Silence

He smiled at the world, not to change or to fix,
But witness its turning, no heed for its tricks.
No creatures to free, no Curtain left to part,
Just breath in his lungs and a listening heart.

No final pronouncement, nor elegant note,
No history's verdict, nor memoir to quote.
The power had faded, the falsehoods ran dry,
When Fox questioned with a wondering of *why?*

End the tale; start the trail.

EPILOGUE
THE PATH FORWARD

The forest now sleeps, yet its stillness can lie.
For the Curtains return when no one asks Why?
Chains sometimes grow soft and the bars turn too kind,
And close without warning around any mind.

Fox left no throne filled and he ordained no king.
Just embers to nurture and questions you bring.
The flame now is yours, hidden, stubborn, and near
To guard in the calm, and still live through the fear.

Use it when others' words grow polished and sweet.
Feed it when comfort causes sparks to retreat.
Walk where the brambles puncture, still poised to tear;
For thorns reveal truths about what hides in there.

Fox left behind no orders, no flags, no bind,
Just a pawprint, a whisper, a path to find.

ABOUT THE AUTHOR

Jonathan is a truth-seeker who has spent years walking the Sly-Path between observed systems and personal revelation. A graduate of the University of Tampa, his professional life as a financial fraud investigator and paralegal provided how power structures operate, protect themselves, and hide the truth in plain sight.

The Fox Who Wondered Why is the direct result of that journey. He wrote it not as a simple critique, but as a coded field guide and a testament; a political animal fable forged from lived experience. His aim is to arm readers with questions, not just answers, and to offer a flame of recognition to those who feel the unseen bars of their own cages.

When not writing, Jonathan tends to a small circle of real conversations and the quiet, radical work of paying attention. He believes the most courageous act is to ask "Why?" and that the truest freedom is found not in escape, but in seeing the labyrinth clearly.

www.ingramcontent.com/pod-product-compliance
Lightning Source LLC
LaVergne TN
LVHW020928090426
835512LV00020B/3254